15.95

Advancing Invitational Thinking

Edited by

John M. Novak

ADVANCING INVITATIONAL THINKING
Edited by John M. Novak

Copyright 1992 by John M. Novak

Published by
   Caddo Gap Press
   3145 Geary Boulevard
   Suite 275
   San Francisco, California 94118

In cooperation with the
   International Alliance for Invitational Education
   School of Education
   Curry Building
   The University of North Carolina at Greensboro
   Greensboro, North Carolina 27412

Price - $15.95

ISBN 1-880192-02-0
Library of Congress Catalog Card Number 92-073151

Contents

Dedication

To Linda Novak and Natalie Novak, who continue to advance invitational thinking through their loving and creative ways of summoning the best from life.

Preface

Books get written because people with energy have something to say and want to find ways to share and sharpen their thinking. These people also need resources to transform their thinking into words on a printed page. This book is no exception to this energetic-resource connection.

The contributors to this volume are artful practitioners and theoreticians of invitational education who decided not to "rust on their laurels." In the process of sharing and extending their own experiences, they have enabled new connections to be made between invitational education and a variety of innovative programs and projects. They also know that we have only touched the tip of the iceberg on the invitational possibilities surrounding us.

Possibilities need resources to be made into actualities. In order for this book to be published, a creative and caring combination of policies, places, programs, and people had to be brought together.

First, in terms of policies, the International Alliance for Invitational Education's policy to seek ways to advance invitational thinking was the impetus for this project. This book, plus the new *Journal of Invitational Theory and Practice*, are examples of this policy in action.

Next, certain environments encourage inviting research and practice. Brock University and its Faculty of Education are such places. I feel fortunate to be part of an inviting community of scholars. The University's Release Time Program was especially important in enabling me to have the opportunity to bring this book together.

Finally, some particular people have been able to provide the inspiration, consolation, and perspiration necessary for developing invitational thinking. Although I cannot possibly thank each individual who has helped us advance invitational thinking, I do think the following individuals deserve special recognition: Terry Boak, Kris Kirkwood, Vic Cicci, and Don Dworet for their administrative and personal encouragement; Veronica Ellis, Larry and Jane Evans, Gord Hamilton, Tom McArthur, and Pam Rogers for their professional expertise in applying invitational principles; Cynthia Peterson, Phyllis Stanley, and Rosemary Young for their collegial support; Joyce Garrett, David Sherrill, Tommie Radd, and Melvin Lang for their continued work with our American Educational Research Association Special Interest Group; and Alan H. Jones of Caddo Gap Press for being an example of an inviting publisher. Thank you all for enabling the conversation about invitational education to continue.

--John M. Novak

Introduction

Chapter 1
Introducing
Invitational Thinking

By John M. Novak and Phyllis Stanley

a. 君相寺看前, 它相好起前

Educators are being bombarded with mandates to do more, do it better (usually with less), and do it even faster. Being hit from all sides, with often contradictory messages, they can easily feel confused, overwhelmed, frustrated, and discounted. It is easy to lose sight of defensible educational purposes, programs, and processes. Thus, educators seek a defensible position that will enable them to respond to these educational urgencies in a caring and productive manner. What is needed is a theory of practice, a thoughtful way of conceptualizing and going about that which is worthwhile doing.

Invitational education, as a theory of practice, is an attempt to provide an integrative framework for constructing environments and cultures that extend and evaluate intentional messages that affirm the uniqueness, possibilities, and dignity of all involved in the educative process. Originating in the book *Inviting School Success* (Purkey, 1978), and being refined and extended in other books (Purkey & Novak, 1984; Wilson, 1986; Purkey & Strahan, 1986; Purkey & Schmidt, 1987; Purkey & Novak, 1988; Purkey & Schmidt, 1990; Purkey & Stanley, 1991), and carefully studied in dissertations (Inglis, 1976; Lambeth, 1980; Stehle, 1981; Amos, 1985; Radd, 1988) and philosophical papers (Novak, 1984; 1985; 1986; 1988; 1990; McLaren, 1986), thinking about educational practice in invitational terms has generated an International Alliance for Invitational Education with more that 1,100 members, an American Educational Research Association Special Interest Group, and an Annual International Conference.

Using a theory of practice perspective, invitational educators are committed to developing an integrative and self-correcting framework. This volume, commissioned by the International Alliance for Invitational Education, is an attempt to re-examine the foundations of invitational education, and apply it to different areas of the school curriculum, administrative practices, higher education, and counseling in order to see how the basic ideas of the inviting approach can connect with, modify, and be modified by other areas of educational practice.

The authors in this volume were asked to practice reflective invitational thinking. They were requested to show how invitational thinking could be connected with another area of educational concern and to explain how invitational thinking might be refined and extended as a result of this connection. Let's briefly look at the invitational connections made by the contributors to this volume.

Foundational Issues

Avoiding Erosion in the Foundations
of Invitational Education:
The Seven Deadly Sins of Self-Concept Theory

In this first foundational chapter, William Watson Purkey argues for the importance of understanding the two interlocking foundations of invitational education, the perceptual tradition and self-concept theory. Without a solid understanding of the foundations, invitational educators will sound like romantic rudderless rhetoricians who lack the depth and coherence necessary to fully articulate the subtlety and complexity of the inviting process. Purkey then points out seven "sins" of self-concept theorizing that warrant the attention of invitational educators. Perhaps the most important of these areas of concern are the "sins" of simplification and immutability. n. 不可以化   n. 簡化

The important points here are that we do not easily or radically change views of who we are and how we fit in the world, because we are always motivated to maintain, protect, and enhance our self-concept. This inner motive is a given and a fundamental part of all we do. External motivation is an oxymoron that makes it even more difficult to get at the person in the process. However, although this fundamental internal motivation cannot be reduced to outside forces, it can be invited forth. Thus, people are always participants in their own growth and sources of messages for others' development. To ignore perceiving invitations from the perspective of the participant is to miss the point of inviting.

Cooperative Learning and Invitational Education: Similarities and Differences

Invitational education claims that cooperation is one of its essential foundations. In this chapter, Lisa Marie Beardsley and George M. Jacobs compare and contrast invitational education and cooperative learning and show how both differ from, and have problems being implemented in, the traditional classroom. They argue that invitational education and cooperative learning, in contrast to the traditional education, emphasize not only academic learning, but also personal and social learning; depend on the social construction of knowledge; use students and other sources of knowledge; and see the process as an integral part of the product. Invitational education provides the big picture and the philosophical perspective, while cooperative learning gives educators empirical support and developed strategies.

In an interesting turn at the end of this chapter, the authors point out some implications from feminist pedagogy for cooperative/invitational education. It might be that a judicious combination of the latter two is necessary to overcome the implicit patriarchal values that are often unconsciously accepted in traditional classrooms. This feminist turn opens up many questions about how schools may be unintentionally disinviting development in all of its participants through a limited and unreflective perspective on gender possibilities.

Curriculum Applications

Invitational and Multicultural Perspectives

A strength of invitational education is that it can start small and be optimistic about possibilities. A weakness, as pointed out by Charlotte Reed, is that it runs the risk of being perceived as that "wonderful, non-threatening, feel-good approach to education" that glosses over important commitments, especially those dealing with the education of diverse populations. Thus this chapter deals with the compatibility of invitational and multicultural perspectives.

Invitational and multicultural education share much overlap in terms of goals, curriculum possibilities, teaching styles, and emphases in learning, methods, and evaluation. What is necessary for invitational educators, however, is to examine their basic values and cultural orientations. A subtle but persistent monocultural undertone is disinviting in process and consequences to an ever-growing portion of the school population. To be truly inviting is to have a united commitment to the educative process and build on the uniqueness and diversity of all the members of the school community. To do otherwise is to seriously limit cooperation and the development of our shared human possibilities.

Invitational Theory:
Applications in Physical Education

For a great many people, physical education is a negative experience that they elect not to repeat. In the United States and Canada, this negative reaction is often manifested in schools by students choosing not to select physical education as a high school elective. Building on the research that looks at the needs and expectations of children with regard to physical education, John Kearns points out seven incentive conditions that have to be considered in creating inviting programs. Without a proper structuring for independence, power, affiliation, excellence, aggression, stress, and success, phys. ed. fizzes out.

Moving from research to practice, this chapter looks at a specific physical education program that builds on the inviting approach. A live model of invitational thinking in action is provided by showing how research results from physical education research can be translated into inviting practices. The results are an impressive increase in the number of students choosing to be actively involved in physical education.

Administrative Practices

Nurturing Personally and Professionally
Inviting Behaviors
through a Clinical Supervision Model

One of the key school issues for the theory and practice of invitational education is how do administrators evaluate teachers from an inviting perspective. Based on an extensive review of the literature on teacher effectiveness and invitational education and their own validated research, John Van Hoose and David Strahan describe the development and use of their Inviting Teaching

Observation Instrument (ITOI). Their research analysis and instrument point out that inviting teacher behavior is also effective teaching behavior.

Going beyond the mere provision of an evaluation instrument, the authors also show how the qualities of the inviting stance (trust, intentionality, respect, and optimism) provide a basis for personally and professionally inviting supervisory behavior. Again, taking their thoughts further into practice, they provide administrators with a collegial and flexible Teacher Improvement Process (TIP). This realistic mechanism for guiding supervisory efforts is a solid example of inviting research.

Invitational Leadership

How do invitational leaders effect change that goes below the surface and gets at the deep structures of schooling? In this chapter, Dean Fink uses the four pillars of invitational education to show how inviting yourself and others personally and professionally provides a sound operating framework for proactive administrators. Arguing that inviting administrators not only do things right, they also do the right things, Fink provides a systematic and substantive way to get at the things worth doing.

In terms of inviting yourself personally, it is imperative for inviting administrators to have a vision capable of being articulated. However, in dealing with others, it is also important that this articulation of vision includes the voices of those involved with implementing educational undertakings. Being professionally inviting to oneself involves judicious use of action research. Inviting others focuses on how to create a "moving" school by use of a collaborative school growth plan. Using a vast array of recent literature on change theory and leadership behavior, this chapter is a rich resource for the artful orchestration of administrative responsibilities.

Implications for Higher Education

An Analysis of Adult Cognitive-Developmental Theory and Invitational Theory

Invitational education is about intentionally developing human beings. If this is the case, then it is particularly important for invitational educators, both personally and professionally, to be informed about and connect invitational and cognitive-developmental theory. In this chapter, Dorothy S. Russell points out similarities and differences between the two approaches. In addition, she suggests some practical ways to integrate these theories for educators working with adults.

In terms of theoretical similarities, Russell points out that both invitational education and cognitive-developmental approaches are optimistic about possibilities, involve interaction with environments, and require reflection. Differences involve the cognitive-developmentalists' focus on stages and their use of constructive mismatch. Thus, although development is the goal of both approaches, they appear to have a different emphasis on challenge and support. Structuring challenging approaches in a supportive environment through such activities as role-taking and peer-tutoring are two ways to integrate inviting development for adults.

The Intentionally Inviting College

How do you create and sustain a challenging and supportive environment for adults? Betty L. Siegel, president of Kennesaw State College, describes the inviting process used to enable her institution to be designated as one of the United States' top twenty colleges "on the move." This movement came by way of a creative use of a strategic inviting plan.

Focusing on having her administrative team use an inviting

model for planning, Kennesaw developed a mission statement that connected excellence and access. Positive opportunities for faculty and students were promoted through such innovations as the Freshman Experience and the Leadership Program. Kennesaw also strengthened diversity by strong recruitment of minority faculty and students and by restructuring the physical and academic environments to better accommodate non-traditional students. Future plans include building more connections with business and other educational groups. This chapter is a moving example of the transformative possibilities of invitational thinking.

Inviting Others and Yourself

Invitational Theory and Counseling

At times, the basic concepts of invitational education seem so intuitively obvious that it is difficult to critically examine them. Counseling, however, provides a more intensive setting, where fundamental ideas are continually tested and refined. In this chapter, William B. Stafford analyzes the intentionality needed by counselors as a way to modify the anatomy of an invitation.

Building on the idea that trust provides the broad supportive base for invitational education and counseling, Stafford interrogates the quality of intentionality necessary to demonstrate and sustain trust in a counseling relationship. Since intentionality is a deep-seated purpose that provides the basis for specific intentions, the commitment to articulate and examine the fundamental purposes of an inviting relationship is a responsibility for all who choose to be intentionally inviting. Invitational thinking is not for the weak of heart, mind, and purpose. It presupposes a commitment to be proactive, thoughtful, and trustworthy, along with an honesty in examining these basic commitments.

Inviting Things To Do in the Privacy of Your Own Mind

Inviting applies not only to others, but also to oneself. In this chapter, Paula Helen Stanley shows how core assumptions and internal dialogue affect a person's life decisions. Using the work of Meichenbaum, Beck, and Ellis, she points out thirteen cognitive distortions that seriously limit the development of a healthy quality of personal life.

Moving beyond merely avoiding the negative, this chapter also describes nine positive things an intentionally-inviting person may choose to do. What is stressed here is that our relationship with ourself is also subject to the requirements and responsibilities of a "doing with" relationship. In other words, all the thinking and sensitivity we use with others is also necessary in dealing with the privacy of our own minds. Our personal thoughts and their underlying beliefs are an important part of the inviting process.

Now that the groundwork has been laid for advancing invitational thinking, it is time to go to the primary sources. We are sure you will find the upcoming chapters insightful, provocative, and delightfully divergent. There is a brief synthesis at the end to show the unity in this diversity.

References

Amos, L. W. (1968). Professionally and personally inviting teacher practices as related to affective course outcomes reported by dental hygiene students. Unpublished doctoral dissertation, University of North Carolina-Greensboro.

Inglis, S. C. (1976). The development and validation of an instrument to assess teacher invitations and teacher effectiveness as reported by students in a technical and general post-secondary setting. Unpublished doctoral dissertation, University of Florida, Gainesville.

Lambeth, C. R. (1980). Teacher invitations and effectiveness as reported by secondary students in Virginia. Unpublished doctoral dissertation, University of Virginia, Charlottesville.

McLaren, P. (1986). Interrogating the conceptual roots of Invitational Education—A review of Purkey and Novak's *Inviting School Success*. *Interchange, 17,* 90-95.

Novak, J. M. (1984). Revisioning invitational education. *Resources in Education.* (ERIC Document No. ED 234 283).

Novak, J. M. (1985). Invitational teaching for mere mortals .Paper presented at the American Educational Research Association, Chicago.

Novak, J. M. (1986). New directions with invitational education: Moving with McLaren from interrogation to conversation. *Interchange, 17,* 96-99.

Novak, J. M. (1988). Teaching for life: An inviting approach. *Monographs in Education*: University of Manitoba. XIX, 53-61.

Novak, J. M. (1990). Advancing constructive education. In R. Neimeyer and G. Neimeyer (editors), *Advances in personal construct psychology,* (225-247). New York: JAI Press.

Purkey, W. W., & Novak, J. M. (1984). *Inviting school success: A self-concept approach to teaching and learning,* (second edition). Belmont, CA: Wadsworth Publishing Company.

Purkey, W. W., & Schmidt, J. J. (1987). *The inviting relationship: An expanded perspective for professional counseling.* Englewood Cliffs, NJ: Prentice-Hall, Inc.

Purkey, W. W., & Schmidt, J. J. (1987). *Invitational learning for counseling and development.* Ann Arbor, MI: The University of Michigan, ERIC/CAPS.

Purkey, W. W., & Stanley, P. H. (1991). *Invitational teaching, learning and living.* Washington, DC: National Education Association Library.

Purkey, W. W., and Strahan, D. (1987). *Positive discipline: A pocketful of ideas.* Columbus, OH: National Middle School Association.

Radd, T. R. (1988). The effects of *Grow With Guidance* on self-concept as learner and teacher self-concept. Unpublished doctoral dissertation, University of Akron, Ohio.

Stehle, C. F. (1981). Invitational learning: A case study of the implementation of the sustained silent reading (SSR) program within the junior high school classroom. Unpublished doctoral dissertation, University of Rochester, NY.

Wilson, J. H. (1986). *The invitational elementary classroom.* Springfield, IL: Charles C Thomas.

Foundational
Issues

Chapter 2
Avoiding Erosion in the Foundations of Invitational Education
The Seven Deadly Sins of Self-Concept Theory

By William Watson Purkey

Invitational education is based on two interlocking foundations: The Perceptual Tradition and Self-Concept Theory. These two foundations, reinforced by decades of scholarly research and writing, give substance and support for invitational education. Without these foundations, invitational education would lose its stability and credibility. Foundations of self-concept theory must be constantly inspected for erosion. A brief overview of the modern history of self-concept theory will explain why this is so.

At the beginning of the present century, there was a tremendous amount of interest in self-concept theory. For example, when William James wrote his classic, *Principles of Psychology* (1890), his chapter on "The Consciousness of Self" was the longest of the two volumes. From this high point of interest, research and writing on self concept took a dramatic decline.

Although the erosion of interest in self-concept was encouraged, and even cheered, by behavioristically-oriented scholars who demanded quantification and concrete proof, the gradual neglect cannot be laid at their door. The most likely reason for the erosion was the helter-skelter, undisciplined, hit-or-miss nature of much of the research and writing in the area. In attempting to deal with a complex but subtle concept, self-concept theorists became either too vague, too mystical, or too simplistic. Thus, their writings were often characterized by theoretical and methodological errors, lack of intellectual rigor, and radical individualism. Self-esteem, self-image, self-concept, and self-report were often used interchangeably, with scant regard for an invariant vocabulary. In sum, self-concept theorists became their own worst enemies.

Now there is a fresh and exciting resurgence of interest in self-concept as a legitimate object of investigation (Beane, 1991; Byrne, 1984, 1987; Hansford & Hattie, 1982; Marsh, Byrne & Shavelson, 1988). There is growing recognition that what people think about themselves internally has a profound influence on what they do externally.

Unfortunately, because earlier misconceptions regarding self-concept have not been cleared up, many of the same errors that led to the decline of scientific interest in self-concept theory in the first part of this century are again appearing. As Hansford and Hattie (1982) suggest, literature on self-concept continues to be a "somewhat ill-disciplined field" (p. 124).

The purpose of this paper is to add discipline to self-concept theory by pointing out (with obvious overstatement) seven deadly sins. By identifying these sins, it is hoped that proponents of invitational education will avoid them in their personal and professional functioning. The seven "sins" are:

1. The "sin" of reification.
2. The "sin" of causation.
3. The "sin" of correlation.
4. The "sin" of simplification.
5. The "sin" of self report.
6. The "sin" of proliferation.
7. The "sin" of immutability.

It will be useful to consider these seven deadly sins in turn.

1. The "Sin" of Reification

This hypothetical construct called " self-concept" is not an "object" or "thing" as such. Rather, it is a continually active and incredibly complex **process** of perceiving and interpreting one's own personal existence. It is the self-concept, not any "real" self, that is the focus of study. Some recent writers and researchers overlook the fact that the very nature of self-concept is a continuing philosophical question. To give this theoretical construct concreteness is misleading and counter-productive.

As Patterson (1961) explained, "The self-concept is, by definition, a phenomenological concept. It is the self as seen by the experiencing individual" (p. 157). The use of self-concept is best employed in attempting to understand the perceptual world of the individual human being. Misplaced concreteness and treating the concept as a tangible object in itself takes away from this understanding.

2. The "Sin" of Causation

Perhaps the most common mistake made by self-concept theorists is to view self as the antecedent of behavior. In professional journals, such statements as "the person is misbehaving **because** of a negative self-concept" are common. A better explanation is that the misbehaving person has learned to see himself or herself as troublesome and is behaving accordingly.

As noted earlier, a person's self-concept is a complex and continuously active perceptual process; it is what the individual believes to be true about his or her personal existence. As such, it serves to guide behavior and enables the individual to assume a particular role or stance in life. Rather than the **initiator** of activity, self concept **guides** the direction of behavior. This process has been explained in detail elsewhere (Purkey, 1970; Purkey & Novak,

1984; Purkey & Schmidt, 1987).

By analogy, the person's self-concept serves as a sort of gyro-compass, pointing to the "true north" of a person's direction in life and influencing the direction of behavior. Shavelson, Hubner, and Stanton (1976) have aptly referred to self-concept as a "moderator variable." This moderator variable approach is more defensible than viewing self-concept as responsible for causing behavior or as the executive agent of the human personality.

3. The "Sin" of Correlation

In numerous research reports, causation is erroneously assumed from correlation. For example, when researchers discover that low academic grade-point averages correlate with low scores on self-concept measures, they conclude that low self-concept is the **cause** of poor grades. While this may be the case, it is difficult to prove because of the nature of correlational measures. It would be equally logical to conclude that poor grades are the **cause** of low self-concept. In fact, both processes could be caused by other unrecognized variables. Each human exists in an "open" perceptual system where everything is intertwined and where a myriad of events, internal and external, are affecting everything else all the time. It is a scientific fallacy to assume causation from correlation.

4. The "Sin" of Simplification

A major reason for the apparent failure of many innovative programs designed to quickly "build," "shape," "enhance," or "develop" positive self-concepts in individuals is the tendency to overlook the tremendously complex, multifaceted, and conservative nature of a person's self-concept. People who have learned over a long period of time to view themselves in essentially negative ways are not likely to change readily. Whether a self concept is psychologically healthy or unhealthy, productive or unproductive, the person clings to his or her self-concept and behaves accordingly.

A number of research studies have indicated that students who have learned to expect failure are likely to sabotage their own efforts when they meet unexpected success (Aronson & Carlsmith, 1962; Curtis, Zanna, & Campbell, 1975; Haan, 1963; Mettee, 1971). As early as 1952, Jersild concluded that students are active in maintaining their self-pictures "even if by misfortune the picture is a false and unhealthy one" (p. 14).

The tendency toward stability and predictability in a person's self-perception is a necessary quality of social life. If people changed suddenly and unpredictably, organized society would be impossible. Most programs designed to "build" self-concepts quickly and simply ("a summer program," a "two-week work-shop," a "weekend retreat," "a course offered 4th period on Thursdays") usually fail because they have oversimplified the incredible complexity of self-concept and do not recognize that conservatism is a vital tendency of the human personality. Changes in self-concept tend to take place slowly and grudgingly.

5. The "Sin" of Self-Report

A fifth "sin" of self-concept theory is the naive assumption that **self-report** is the same as **self-concept**. Clearly, they are distinct and should not be used interchangeably.

The validity and reliability of what individuals profess about themselves depend on many factors, such as feelings of trust, the setting in which the disclosure takes place, or the ability to verbalize complex personal feelings. As Combs (1962) explained, " the self-concept is what an individual believes to be true of his or her personal existence. The self-report, on the other hand, is what a person is ready, willing, able, or can be tricked into saying about oneself...clearly, these concepts are by no means the same" (p. 52). While self-report and self-concept may at times overlap, they should not be confused with one another.

The vast majority of studies purporting to investigate self-concept are, in fact, based on self-report rating scales. Writers and researchers who rely on self-report would improve the accuracy of their reporting by using the term "professed" in defining what they mean by their use of the term self-concept.

6. The "Sin" of Proliferation

Thanks to the growing interest in self-concept, a proliferation of tests, inventories, surveys, and questionnaires are appearing, almost all claiming to measure self-concept and almost all relying on self-report. Unfortunately, the great majority of these measures have not been subjected to validation procedures. Their reliability and validity are unknown, and therefore should be considered suspect.

Rather than continue to multiply the number of self-concept measures, it would seem better to agree on construct definition, substantiate the construct validity of a few measures, and develop a degree of standardization of instruments among self-concept researchers so that data collected by one researcher could be compared with data collected by others. This process would allow for replication and the orderly development of valid and reliable self-concept measures.

7. The "Sin" of Immutability

Earlier in this paper, the notion was presented that self-concept is remarkably conservative and tends to resist change. This resistance to change is understandable when change is seen as a threat to one's perceived existence. From a phenomenal viewpoint, to ask a person to change is to ask that person to be someone else. Fortunately, when opportunities to change are seen by the experiencing individual as an invitation, rather than a threat, then changes are most likely to occur. As new experiences are presented to the individual, as invitations from significant others are received, accepted, and acted upon, changes do occur. Gradually, new ideas about oneself filter into the perceptual world of the perceiving person, while old ideas fade away. This continuous process of selecting and evaluating, accepting and rejecting perceptions, creates flexibility in human personality and allows for psychological development.

The theoretical reason for new ideas being assimilated and old ideas being expelled is that each person appears to have a basic need to maintain, protect, and enhance one's self-concept by obtaining positive self-regard and regard from others. This basic human desire for enhancement is a tremendous "given" for proponents of invitational education. Rather than focusing on ways to "motivate" people, proponents of invitational education can assume that the basic motivating force is already in place; that at heart each human wants to become what he or she is capable of being. Change is most likely accomplished in an environment that consistently and patiently invites the process of realizing human potential.

Conclusion

This article has presented the "seven deadly sins of self-concept theory" with the goal that proponents of invitational education will recognize these sins and seek to avoid them in their work. Like any structure, invitational education will stand or fall based on the firmness of its foundations. Because self-concept theory provides a basis for invitational education, it is important for proponents of invitational education to recognize flaws in thinking about this hypothetical construct.

References

Aronson, E., & Carlsmith, J. (1962). Performance expectancy as a determinant of actual performance. *Journal of Abnormal and Social Psychology.*, 65, 178-182.

Beane, J. A. (1991). Sorting out the self-esteem controversy, *Educational Leadership*, September, 25-30.

Byrne, B. M. (1984). The general/academic self-concept nomological network: A review of construct validation research. *Review of Educational Research*, 54, 427-456.

Byrne, B. M. (1986). Self concept/academic achievement relations: An investigation of dimensionality, stability, and causality. *Canadian Journal of Behavioral Science.*, 18, 173-186.

Byrne, B. M., & Shavelson, R. J. (1987). Adolescent self-concept: Testing the assumption of equivalent structure across gender. *American Educational Research Journal*, 24, 365-385.

Combs, A. W. (1962) A self in chaos. A review of Wylie, R. C., The self concept: A critical survey of pertinent research literature. *Contemporary Psychology*, 7, 53-54.

Curtis, R., Zanna, M., & Campbell, W. (1975). Sex, fear of success, and the perceptions and performance of law school students. *American Educational Research Journal.*, 12, 287-297.

Haan, R. R. (1963). *Accelerated learning programs.* New York: Center for Applied Research in Education.

Hansford, B. C., & Hattie, J. A. (1982). The relationship between self and achievement/performance measures. *Review of Educational Research*, 52, 123-142.

James, W. (1890) *Principles of Psychology.* Two Volumes. Magnolia, MA: Peter Smith, Publishers.

Jersild, A. T. (1952). *In Search of Self.* New York: Columbia University.

Marsh, H. W., Byrne, B. M., & Shavelson, R. J. (1988). A multifaceted academic self-concept: Its hierarchical structure and its relation to academic achievement. *Journal of Educational Psychology*, 80, 366-380.

Mettee, D. R. (1971). Rejection of unexpected success as a function of the negative consequences of accepting success, *Journal of Personality and Social Psychology*, 71, 332-341.

Patterson, C. H. (1961). The self in recent Rogerian Theory, *Psychologia,* IV(3), September, 157.

Purkey, W. W. (1970). *Self concept and school achievement.* Englewood Cliffs, NJ: Prentice-Hall.

Purkey, W. W. (1978) *Inviting school success.* Belmont, CA: Wadsworth Publishing.

Purkey, W. W., & Novak, J. (1984). *Inviting school success: A self concept approach to teaching and learning.* Belmont, CA: Wadsworth Publishing.

Purkey, W. W., & Schmidt, J. J. (1987). *The inviting relationship: An expanded perspective for professional counseling.* Englewood Cliffs, NJ: Prentice Hall.

Shavelson, R., Hubner, J., & Stanton, G. (1976). Self concept: Validation of construct interpretations. *Review of Educational Research,* 46, 407-441.

Chapter 3
Cooperative Learning and Invitational Education: Similarities and Differences

By Lisa Marie Beardsley and George M. Jacobs

Links and distinctions between invitational education and cooperative learning have been discussed elsewhere (Jacobs & Ilola, 1990; 1991), but are further clarified in this chapter. The format of this discussion will be to first define invitational education and cooperative learning. Next, similarities and differences are considered. Some common obstacles to implementation in schools that these two perspectives may face are outlined. Finally, we suggest greater awareness of linkages with other areas of pedagogy.

Definition of Invitational Education

The classic definition of invitational education is found in *Inviting School Success* (Purkey & Novak, 1984). Drawing major inspiration from humanistic learning theory and approaches for counseling, invitational education emphasizes the need for teachers and other participants in the school environment to "invite students to see themselves as able, valuable, and self-directing" (p. xiii).

Individuals, teachers in particular, may function at one of four levels in their day to day interactions with students. The lowest level is to be intentionally disinviting and the next to lowest is to be unintentionally disinviting. The second highest is to be unintentionally inviting and the highest level of function is to be intentionally inviting. Obviously, the most desirable level of functioning that teachers as persons and professionals should strive for is to be consistently intentionally inviting. In fact, it is proposed that it is a teacher's professional responsibility to be inviting in a deliberate and consistent manner.

This is only possible when the teacher develops the "inviting stance." This means that the teacher perceives himself or herself, as well as others, in a basically positive manner. A norm of behavior that is stable over time is the result of these positive self and other perceptions. This baseline stance guides the teacher in the sending or not sending of invitations, responding to students' acceptance or nonacceptance of invitations, and management of the classroom in general.

Purkey and Novak outline eight steps to creating the conditions for learning. Creation of the ideal learning environment and the interpersonal context "frees the student to learn" (1984, p. 55). To do so, the teacher must develop and elicit students' trust, demonstrate personal interest in each student, read situations appropriately, make invitations attractive, insure delivery of messages, negotiate invitations, handle rejection, and follow up on invitations. This process is based on reflection.

Invitational education is perhaps best described as a theory of process and practice. It is a cyclical and interactive model of learning and teaching. It involves teachers and students both being personally and professionally inviting with each other and with themselves.

"Teachers have a moral obligation to their students to take care of themselves" (1984, p. 73). Certainly, a healthy and well rested teacher is better prepared to resolve the challenges each day brings.

Examples of being professionally inviting with oneself are to write for publications (as we are doing with this chapter) or to attend professional meetings and meet with colleagues who share similar concerns. To be professionally inviting with students, the teacher might listen as a particularly timid student first rehearses the following day's oral presentation in the empty classroom after school.

It is also a constructivist model of teaching and learning (Novak, 1990). Inviting relationships and communities of inquiry are constructed by equals and participants, students and teachers together. Novak describes education as the process of getting smarter about important things, and pedagogy as attending to the factors that enable this to occur. Invitational education is a cooperative activity, a "doing with" relationship "emphasizing the choices, mutuality, and possibilities implicit in educational development as a social practice" (p. 240).

A final key feature of invitational education is its emphasis on the importance of the social context of education. The social context of education refers to interactions among students, teachers, and schools. It consists of the places, policies, and programs of the bureaucracy of the educational system (Purkey & Novak, 1984, p. 2). In order for invitational educational to be truly effective, it must be institutionalized and rewarded within the larger educational context.

Stepping back to view the larger context is not unique to invitational education. The Northwest Regional Educational Laboratory (1984) summarizes research on effective schooling practices along similar lines. Research findings are synthesized and grouped into three main areas: (1) classroom characteristics and practices, (2) school characteristics and practices, and (3) district characteristics and practices. What distinguishes invitational education is its strong foundation in humanistic philosophy rather than empiricism. Even though the school district or the administrators or the school may be less than ideal (probably the rule, not the exception), invitational education inspires teachers to foster the professional and personal growth of those connected with their classrooms. As such, it might be characterized as a "salt of the earth" model of education. It flavors the daily bread of education. More importantly, it also provides a philosophical basis on which to ground teaching behaviors.

Definition of Cooperative Learning

The general area of cooperative learning draws on many learning theories (Jacobs, 1990; Slavin, 1989) and encompasses a number of different applications. Thus, arriving at a commonly accepted definition is highly problematic. It is also known by a variety of names: "cooperative learning," "collaborative learning," "peer interactive learning," "team learning," and "peer tutoring" approaches. The core feature is that they all refer to student-student rather than direct teacher-student pedagogical interactions.

Compared to the lecture approach and other traditional modes of instruction, cooperative learning approaches have done well. Numerous studies have, overall, found increased levels of academic achievement, increases in student self-esteem, and increased attendance and reported liking for school (Aronson & Osherow, 1980; Johnson, 1981; Sharan, 1980; Slavin, 1980). The development of positive peer relationships and increases in mutual concern among students have also been reported (Aronson & Osherow, 1980). This was also observed in classrooms that contained racially and culturally different, socially isolated, and handicapped students (Lew *et al.*, 1986; Slavin, 1985, 1987).

How do the results cited above happen? Haphazard interaction is not likely to produce good results. Positive results are the product of interaction structured so that students engage in specific activities. A number of carefully designed studies have been able to tease out which activities are most effective. From these studies, the critical features of cooperative learning have emerged. Davidson (1990, pp. 89) developed two lists of critical attributes of cooperative learning: one which he believes everyone working in the field would agree on; the other with attributes that are integral to some cooperative learning approaches, but not to others.

The criterial attributes he believes are generally agreed upon are: (a) a "task for group discussion and resolution (if possible)," (b) "face-to-face interaction," (c) "an atmosphere of cooperation and mutual helpfulness within each group," and (d) "individual accountability."

Attributes which he believes are central to some cooperative learning approaches, but not others, are: (a) "heterogeneous or random grouping," (b) "explicit teaching of social skills," and (c) "structured mutual interdependence." While interdependence can be obtained in several ways (rewards, tasks, scripts), it is typically structured through rewards, such as assignment of a single group grade.

The Jigsaw method (Aronson *et al.*, 1978) is an example of a method with all the attributes generally agreed upon. A group task is assigned which can only be completed by each member doing his or her own part. Each student is assigned a certain amount of material (task) to first learn (individual accountability) and then teach to peers (face-to-face interaction, mutual helpfulness), using whatever teaching skills he or she has.

Students quickly learn that the success of the group is dependent on the active participation of each group member. There are no free rides, and students are motivated to both do their part, and make sure that others do theirs, too. They also learn that developing and using social skills are an important way to resolve conflicts and promote pleasant group interactions.

The task, individual accountability, face-to-face interaction, and mutual helpfulness can also be scripted. These scripts may require students to engage in certain behaviors, tasks, or specified roles, such as being the Summarizer, Elaborator, or Writer (Dansereau, 1984, 1987; Jacobs & Zhang, 1989; Ilola, 1991).

These scripts usually provide opportunities for students to link their experiences and feelings to the material they are learning (Hythecker, Dansereau, & Rocklin, 1988). We have described how to use the criterial features of cooperative learning to structure student interaction elsewhere (Ilola, Power, & Jacobs, 1989)

A large body of literature documents the applicability of cooperative learning techniques to a variety of subjects and levels, from elementary (Palincsar & Brown, 1986) through collegiate instruction (Dansereau, 1987). It has been used with language arts and writing (Slavin, 1980), reading (Au & Kawakami, 1984), high school mathematics (Berg, 1992; Davidson, 1990), science (Hassard, 1990); computer instruction (Johnson, Johnson, & Stanne, 1986); ESL/EFL (Jacobs & Zhang, 1989), and crosscultural interaction training (Ilola, 1991).

Similarities and Differences

Both invitational education and cooperative learning are general models which are suitable for use in any subject or at any level. Also, they both share the same goals of obtaining greater student participation, fostering horizontal rather than vertical relationships, and recognizing the importance of the social context of learning and the value of individual students.

However, each varies in the degree of emphasis on the fundamental issues that distinguish them from the traditional classroom. These variations are summarized in Table 1.

Practitioners of invitational education reject what Purkey and Novak (1984, p. 90) label the "efficient factory" model of education. As in any efficient factory, products are mass produced, control is centralized, and workers are slot-filling functionaries. Naturally, the physical arrangement of the classroom reflects the educational assumptions of the teacher. In a typical scene in a traditional

Table 1
Variations in Emphasis on the Fundamental Issues
That Distinguish Invitational Education and Cooperative Learning
from the Traditional Classroom

	Invitational Education	Cooperative Learning
Greater student participation	Invite students to be responsible, able and valuable; specific student behaviors not systematically defined	Use of structured learning materials and activities that require students to use specific skills or perform certain tasks.
Foster horizontal rather than vertical relationships	All school personnel should be student-centered.	Heterogeneous groupings of students marshalled around a superordinate goal move teachers from information dissemination role.
Social context of learning	Scope of educational arena is global: society, schools, teachers, and students.	Social construction of knowledge is teacher-directed but occurs primarily in student-student interactions.
Value of individual student	Sending and resending of invitational messages tailored to individual student.	Role of an individual's prior knowledge in processing of new learning.

classroom, student desks are in rows, facing the desk of the teacher. The teacher is the focus of attention visually. The teacher is also the source of learning.

Instead, invitational education calls for teachers to perceive students as responsible, capable individuals, and to show them the respect they accordingly deserve by inviting students' full and active participation in the school. It recognizes individual differences and decentralizes control in the classroom.

Similarly, cooperative learning very much urges a restructuring of classroom relations so that students are more actively engaged. This also manifests itself in physical arrangements. For example, student desks may be clustered when students work together on a group assignment.

In a college-level class in which principles of invitational education and cooperative learning were applied, a "Reading Center" became the physical and symbolic hub of student learning (Sherrill *et al.*, 1989). An open file of everyone's written work was maintained in the "Reading Center," a room joining a suite of faculty offices and accessible to students until evening. Each student had a folder in the file which included all assignments. A form was attached to each assignment on which to record the names of those who read that particular paper. Students were requested to write comments to the author of the paper describing reactions, such as what the reader liked the best. They also wrote suggestions to improve the writing or content, or queried about things the reader wished additional elaboration.

Usually, only teachers read students' papers. Requiring the reading and responding to a sample of their classmates' papers helped students become more responsible for their own learning as well as that of their peers. Many students commented on the value of this simple reading requirement (see Sherrill *et al* for a more detailed explanation of this application of invitational education at the university level).

Many approaches to cooperative learning place great emphasis on helping students develop specific social skills necessary to successful interactions. Stanger (1987) believes that successful small group collaboration brings to students a feeling of connection to others. With cooperative learning, the spotlight is no longer on teachers performing for their students. Instead, students spend a lot of time in groups learning with each other. Teachers are still very much part of the cast, but in more of a supporting role, helping students learn from each other, as well as from other sources.

While both invitational education and cooperative learning share the goal of restructuring interactions in the classroom, interactions take place within a broader scope in invitational education. It urges educators to consider the sociological matrix in which students, teachers, and teaching are embedded (Figure 1). The larger picture includes the school district and administrative structure of the school that can potentially support the activities of the classroom. While the relationship between teacher and student is primary, the goal is to reform the entire school. In invitational education, even cafeteria workers and school bus drivers have roles in the inviting school.

Although also concerned with the larger social context and long-term benefits, the scope tends to be tighter in cooperative learning. Some literature has been written for administrators leading a cooperative school (Johnson & Johnson, 1989a), and others have found positive long-term effects in interracial interactions (Schwarzwald & Amir, 1988). However, cooperative learning tends to focus on the type of student behaviors and interactions which account for positive learning outcomes, whether academic or social.

For the sake of highlighting the strength of each, Figure 1 exaggerates a distinction between the two in their scope of focus. Students are in the center of both models. In invitational education, there is a more explicit emphasis on interdependence of parts in "the big picture." The concentric circles are solid lines because this model explicitly defines interdependence between student, teacher, the school, and society.

In cooperative learning, there is a tighter analysis of student interactions. In this model, the teacher orchestrates processes so that student-student interactions are productive. Teacher and students are loosely enclosed in a dotted line which separates the classroom from the rest of the world, because the latter relationship is not always defined in all cooperative learning approaches.

This doesn't mean that cooperative learning has no peripheral vision, nor that invitational education is an overgeneralized and impractical model of education in terms of the day-to-day events of the classroom. Both models are broad in perspective and both incorporate practical strategies that can be used on a daily basis.

While entire schools and groups of teachers are adopting invitational education and cooperative learning—and this is ideal—what makes them both appealing is that they work in individual classrooms even without schoolwide support.

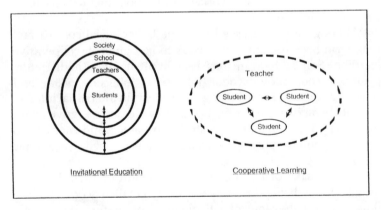

Figure 1. Scope of Interactions in Invitational Education and Cooperative Learning.

Most cooperative learning approaches urge the formation of heterogeneous groups based on characteristics such as ethnicity, gender, past achievement level, and interest. This capitalizes on the variety of social contexts each student represents. Some of the methods which use heterogeneous grouping of students do so to provide students with a mix of perspectives, which in turn reduce the misunderstandings and prejudice which differences easily cause. United by a superordinate learning goal, students work together to arrive at a socially constructed understanding of knowledge.

Some, but not all, approaches to cooperative learning also draw inspiration from humanistic philosophy. Although research findings for all the main approaches show gains on affective variables such as self-esteem and liking for other, the approaches vary greatly in the importance they place on these types of outcomes.

Specific student behaviors which increase learning or interpersonal skills are defined quite systematically in cooperative learning. In invitational education, however, more emphasis is placed on a general tone of positive interpersonal relations between students and teachers. A definition of what a cooperative spirit and sense of belonging are is left to the discretionary judgment of the teacher in the inviting school (Purkey & Novak, 1984, pp. 96-97).

A valuing of the individual student's uniqueness is another similarity of the two approaches. In invitational education, it underlies the sending and resending of invitational messages which are tailored to the individual student. In cooperative learning, it is seen in some of the scripted approaches which recognize the critical role a student's prior knowledge has in meaningful information processing.

Similar Problems

Given the similarities between invitational education and cooperative learning, it is not surprising that they share similar implementation problems. Rich (1990) investigated reasons why teachers are reluctant to implement cooperative learning. Incorporating the work of Palincsar, Stevens, and Gavelek (1988), Rich believes there are two dimensions along which many educators' belief systems and teaching styles conflict with the implementation of cooperative learning. The first dimension concerns how much emphasis schools should place on the personal and social, rather than academic. Teachers who feel that anything not directly related to academics is a waste of time will resist either of the two perspectives on education discussed in this chapter.

Resistance may also arise from assumptions regarding the source, nature, and process of student learning: the teacher alone, or the teacher and interaction with peers. Studies such as that by Bussis, Chittenden, and Amarel (1976) have consistently found that the majority of teachers believe in the traditional kind of vertical classroom structure in which teachers are at the top. Assumptions found in the traditional classroom that cause implementation barriers for invitational education and cooperative learning are summarized in Table 2.

How can these barriers to implementation be removed? Rich and Palincsar *et al.* emphasize the need to educate teachers about the concepts and supporting research underlying the use of peer interaction. In other words, just providing teachers with a series of techniques will not lead to successful realization of educational change if they hold beliefs they perceive to be in conflict with such processes.

The same lesson can be applied to students. All the social engineering that teachers design collapses without collaboration from students. We cannot expect students to adapt successfully to the kinds of innovations that invitational education and cooperative learning entail, if we do not include them in on the thinking which underlies these perspectives on education. To do anything less would be inconsistent with these perspectives themselves. Positive interdependence and individual accountability and the

Table 2
Traditional Classroom Assumptions that Cause Implementation
Problems for Invitational Education and Cooperative Learning

	Traditional Education	Invitational Education and Cooperative Learning
Legitimacy of Personal/Social vs. Academic Learning	Academic is legitimate but personal/social is borderline.	Both are important and legitimate.
Source of Student Learning	Teacher, books, other authorities.	Other students, teachers, other sources.
Nature of Knowledge	Defined by teacher, textbooks, other authorities.	Based on external criteria but socially constructed.
Student Learning	Product	Process

acceptance or rejection of invitations is, ultimately, the result of
student and not teacher cognitions and behaviors. Students must
be as convinced as teachers that the process of learning is integral
to the product.

Why Stop At Two?

A key purpose of this chapter has to been to review these two
perspectives on education and the links between them. Doubtless,
there are links we have missed. Further, we are certain that the
ideas shared by these two perspectives are also shared with others.
For example, in a book on peace education, Reardon (1988) dis-

cusses the complementarity of feminist pedagogy and cooperative learning to peace education. Reardon sees the need for feminist transformation in education and elsewhere because she views patriarchal values as conducive to war and the milieu which generates more war. Cooperative learning is appropriate to peace education, according to Reardon, because it helps people form positive attitudes toward others.

Perhaps someone with a feminist perspective would tell us that we should learn a lesson from our perception of all these similarities. Maybe we are too dualistic in our view of various educational perspectives. In our zeal to categorize, differentiate, and isolate, we have forgotten to integrate, embrace, and make whole (Gilligan, 1982; Penelope & Wolfe, 1983). In a comparison of invitational education, cooperative learning, and feminist pedagogy we found many similarities. All three agree on the inestimable value of the student as an individual, the benefits of horizontal rather than vertical relationships in schools, and the importance of the social context within which education occurs (Jacobs & Ilola, 1991). Each approach has a unique area which does not overlap the others. For example, although feminist pedagogy is not only for females (Annas, 1987), it's most obvious contribution is a clear focus on the needs of females in educational settings (Rosser, 1989; Hall & Sandler, 1982).

Purkey and Novak stress the effect that teachers' perceptions of students have on students' self-concepts. Thus, for example, advocates of invitational education would counsel teachers to avoid behaviors which stereotype females' abilities and futures. Additionally, as discussed above, invitational education is congruent with many aspects of the broad realignment of traditional classroom environments.

Does cooperative learning help eliminate problems females experience in "male" dominated fields? Cooperative learning seems more congenial to female learning styles than do traditional, teacher-fronted instructional formats. Johnson, Johnson, and Stanne

(1986) collected sociometric data regarding the desirability of female work partners in a study that compared cooperative, competitive, and individualistic computer-assisted instruction. Even though males in all three conditions perceived computers as being more of a male domain than did females, students who had worked together in the cooperative condition nominated significantly more female classmates as desirable future work partners than did students in the other two conditions. Their cooperative learning experience increased the perceived status of females in the "male" area of computers. However, in their latest review of research on cooperative learning, Johnson and Johnson (1989, p. 47) found no significant differences in either the achievement or the productivity of females and males in cooperatively, competitively, or individualistically structured classrooms. Perhaps, this finding could be explained by saying that cooperative learning is beneficial to males as well as females.

Another area in which cooperative learning may be hypothesized to aid in removing impediments to full participation by females would be in improving interpersonal relations. Cooperative learning has been found to increase perspective-taking ability and improve relations between disparate groups, e.g., blacks and whites (Johnson & Johnson, 1989b). Thus, cooperative learning might help males better appreciate females' views. To our knowledge, no research review has examined these variables with respect to female-male relations.

Conclusion

Invitational education and cooperative learning are general pedagogical approaches teachers can adopt in their own classrooms, from elementary to collegiate levels. They are compatible with each other and can be used simultaneously. Both reiterate the social construction of knowledge. And in both the process of learning is seen as a fundamental part of the product.

The strength of invitational education lies in the philosophical foundation that can guide the behavior of the teacher as the professional in the joint effort of education. Cooperative learning's strength is that it provides empirically tested methods that teachers can use to structure the student behaviors that promote learning and positive interactions. As such, they can be valuable tools in the inviting teacher's toolbox.

References

Annas, P. J. (1987). Silences: Feminist language research and the teaching of writing. In C. L. Caywood, & G. R. Overing (editors), *Teaching writing: Pedagogy, gender, and equity.* Albany, NY: State University of New York Press.

Aronson, E., Blaney, N., Sikes, J., & Snapp, M. (1978). *The jigsaw classroom.* Beverly Hills, CA: Sage.

Aronson, E., & Osherow, N. (1980). Cooperation, prosocial behavior, and academic performance: Experiments in the desegregated classroom. In L. Bickman, (editor), *Applied Social Psychology Annual,* (Volume 1). Beverly Hills, CA: Sage Publications.

Au, K. H., & Kawakami, A. J. (1984). Vygotskian perspectives on discussion processes in small group reading lessons. In P. L. Peterson, L. C. Wilkinson, & M. T. Hallman, (editors), *The social context of instruction,* (209-225). Orlando, FL: Academic Press.

Berg, K. F. (1992). Structured cooperative learning and achievement in a high school mathematics classroom. Unpublished doctoral dissertation, University of Hawaii, Honolulu.

Bussis, A. M., Chittenden, F., & Amarel, M. (1976). *Beyond surface curriculum.* Boulder, CO: Westview Press.

Dansereau, D. F. (1984, October). Cooperative learning strategies (Revised. 1985). A paper presented at the Conference on Study and Learning Strategies, Texas A & M University.

Dansereau, D. F. (1987). Transfer from cooperative to individual studying. *Journal of Reading, 29,* 614-619.

Davidson, N. (1990). *Cooperative learning in mathematics.* Menlo Park, CA: Addison Wesley.

Gilligan, C. (1982). *In a different voice: Psychological theory and womens' development.* Cambridge, MA: Harvard University Press.

Hall, R. M., & Sandler, B. R. (1982). *The classroom climate: A chilly one for women?* Washington, D.C.: Project on the Status and Education of Women.

Hassard, J. (1990). *Science experiences: Cooperative learning and the teaching of science.* Menlo Park, CA: Addison Wesley.

Hythecker, V. I., Dansereau, D. F., and Rocklin, T. R. (1988). An analysis of the processes influencing the structured dyadic learning environment. *Educational Psychologist, 23,* 23-37.

Ilola, L. M. (1991, April). The use of structured social interaction with the culture-general assimilator to increase cognitive problem solving about intercultural interactions in an ethnically diverse population. Paper presented at the meeting of the American Educational Research Association, Chicago.

Ilola, L. M., Power, K. M., & Jacobs, G. (1989). Structuring student interaction to promote learning. *English Teaching Forum, 27*(3), 12-16.

Jacobs, G. M. (1990, January). Foundations of cooperative learning. Paper presented at the meeting of the Hawaii Educational Research Association, Honolulu.

Jacobs, G. M., & Ilola, L. M. (1990). Disagreement can be inviting: A cooperative learning approach. Honolulu: University of Hawaii at Manoa. (ERIC Document Reproduction Service No. ED 319 738).

Jacobs, G. M., & Ilola, L. M. (1991). A brief look at how feminist pedagogy interrelates with invitational education and cooperative learning. Honolulu: University of Hawaii at Manoa. (ERIC Document Reproduction Service No. ED 332 984).

Jacobs, G. M., & Zhang, S. (1989). Peer feedback in second language writing: Boon or bane. Paper presented at the Annual Meeting of the American Educational Research Association, San Francisco.

Johnson, D. W. (1981). Student-student interaction: The neglected variable in education. *Educational Researcher, 10,* 510.

Johnson, D. W., & Johnson, R. T. (1989a). *Leading the cooperative school.* Edina, MN: Interaction Book Company.

Johnson, D. W., & Johnson, R. T. (1989b). *Cooperation and competition: Theory and research.* Edina, MN: Interaction Book Co.

Johnson, R. T., Johnson, D. W., & Stanne, M. B. (1986). Comparison of computer-assisted cooperative, competitive, and individualistic learning. *American Educational Research Journal, 23*(3), 382-392.

Lew, M., Mesch, D., Johnson, D. W., & Johnson, R. (1986). Positive interdependence, academic and collaborative skills group contingencies, and isolated students. *American Educational Research Journal,* 23(3), 476-488.

Northwest Regional Educational Laboratory. (1984). *Effective schooling practices: a research synthesis.* Portland, OR: Northwest Regional Educational Laboratory.

Novak, J. M. (1990). Advancing constructive education: A framework for teacher education. In G. Neimeyer & R. A. Neimeyer (editors), *Advances in personal construct psychology.* Greenwich, CT: JAI Press.

Palincsar, A. S., & Brown, A. L. (1986). Interactive teaching to promote independent learning from text. *The Reading Teacher,* April, 771-777.

Palincsar, A., Stevens, D., & Gavelek, J. (1988, April). Collaborating in the interest of collaborative learning. Paper presented at the meeting of the American Educational Research Association, New Orleans. (ERIC Document Reproduction Service No. ED 305 169).

Penelope, J., & Wolfe, S. J. (1983). Consciousness as style; style as aesthetic. In B. Thorne, C. Kramarae, & N. Henley (editors), *Language, gender and society.* Rowley, MA: Newbury House.

Purkey, W. W., & Novak, J. M. (1984). *Inviting school success.* (second edition). Belmont, CA: Wadsworth.

Reardon, B. A. (1988). *Comprehensive peace education: Educating for global responsibility.* New York: Teachers College Press.

Rich, Y. (1990). Ideological impediments to instructional innovation: The case of cooperative learning. *Teaching & Teacher Education,* 6, 81-91.

Rosser, S. V. (1989). Warming up the classroom climate for women. *Feminist Teacher,* 4, 8-12.

Schwarzwald, J., & Amir, Y. (1988, August). Long-term effects of school desegregation. Paper presented at the Ninth International Congress of the International Association for Cross Cultural Psychology, Newcastle, Australia.

Sharan, S. (1980). Cooperative learning in small groups: Recent methods and effects on achievement, attitudes, and ethnic relations. *Review of Educational Research,* 50(2), 241-271.

Sherrill, D., Ilola, L. M., Jacobs, G., & Hansen, S. (1989). Inviting participation, awareness, and reflection in educational psychology: a display of student works. Presented at the annual meeting of the American Educational Research Association, San Francisco.

Slavin, R. E. (1980). Cooperative learning. *Review of Educational Research,* 50(2), 315-342.
Slavin, R. E. (1985). An introduction to cooperative learning research. In R. E. Slavin, S. Sharan, S. Kagan, Hertz Lazarowitz, C. Webb, and R. Schmuck (editors), *Learning to cooperate, cooperation to learn,* (515). New York: Plenum.
Slavin, R. E. (1987). Cooperative learning: Can students help students learn? *Instructor,* March, pp. 74-78.
Slavin, R. E. (1989). Cooperative learning and student achievement: Six theoretical perspectives. In M. L. Maehr & C. Ames (editors), *Advances in motivation and achievement: Motivation enhancing environments,* Vol. 6 (pp. 161-177). Greenwich, CT: JAI Press Inc.
Stanger, C.A. (1987). The sexual politics of the one-on-one tutorial approach and collaborative learning. In C. L. Caywood & G. R. Overing (editors), *Teaching writing: Pedagogy, gender, and equity.* Albany, NY: State University of New York Press.

Curriculum
Applications

Chapter 4
Invitational and Multicultural Perspectives:
What Do They Have in Common?

By Charlotte Reed

While much attention has been given to creating inviting schools, little has been done to seriously address the implications of invitational education for multicultural schools, more specifically those schools which include diverse populations of students who are culturally and racially different, exceptional, homeless, poor, or in some other way at risk. Even less has been done to establish the compatibility of invitational and multicultural frameworks for the integration of both in the improvement of schools.

Therefore, the purpose of this chapter is to analyze both philosophical frameworks by defining and comparing the elements of the educative process within each, summarizing the compatibility of the two approaches, discussing the implications of their compatibility, and finally, drawing some conclusions about the need to integrate both approaches into the school restructuring process.

What is Invitational Education?

Invitational education (Purkey, 1978; Purkey & Novak, 1984;

Lewis & Purkey, 1983) is a refreshingly people-oriented theory of practice, designed to refashion schools to be more like families than factories, by addressing the entire school environment and all of its members for the sole purpose of creating a quality of life in schools that is intentionally inviting, exciting, satisfying, and enriching for everyone involved. The ultimate goal is twofold: first, having an improved environment, which is intentionally nurturing and supportive; and second, having improved personal and professional relationships, which causes people to have a greater level of success in the educative process.

Assumptions

Every theory or philosophy has some fundamental beliefs upon which it is based. Invitational education is no exception. Some underlying assumptions of this theory of practice, identified in the invitational literature, include, but are not limited to:

1. Positive self-concept and self-esteem are essential to school success;

2. Education should be a collaborative and cooperative process, emphasizing what you do with students;

3. Invitational functioning becomes a personal and professional mentality or a way of life;

4. Affective development is equally as important as cognitive development; and

5. Invitational education is concerned with the gestalt of educational environments, examining their personnel, facilities, procedures or policies, processes, and programs.

Proponents of invitational education believe that respect for individual uniqueness is essential for positive self-concept development, academic achievement, and ultimately, success in life. The diverse nature of schools, communities, and the larger society makes this kind of respect even more essential.

Based on these and other assumptions, this philosophical approach is antithetical to the metaphor of school as factory, but has strong resonance with the metaphor of school as family, which Purkey and Novak (1984) identified as the "inviting family school." In their model, the school possesses five characteristics that parallel those found in healthy functional families. They are: "respect for individual uniqueness," emphasizing the importance of relating to people as individuals, who bring different knowledge, abilities, and experiences to the environment; "cooperative spirit," emphasizing the importance of working cooperatively for the good of all and avoiding unnecessary competitive practices; "sense of belonging," stressing the relevance of creating a caring environment and developing significant relationships to promote feelings of unity and self-efficacy; "pleasing habitat," stressing the relevance of providing a clean attractive, and safe environment for all to enjoy; and "positive expectations," conveying the significance of possessing positive beliefs about the potential of each person to succeed.

The consistent and reliable presence of these functional family characteristics creates environments and relationships that are based on trust, respect, optimism, and positive intentionality. These environments and relationships are beneficial and invite success.

Invitational theorists (Purkey & Novak, 1984; Lewis & Purkey, 1991; Reed, 1991) reject the metaphor of school as factory, finding some of the related attributes less desirable. Six attributes are related to efficient factory schools:

(1) "Mass production," emphasizing quantity instead of quality minimal standards, and a rigidly administered generic curriculum for all students. Pedagogy is specified and inflexibly controlled.

(2) "A uniform product," emphasizing conformity through mandated minimal competencies and exit skills is sought. Promotion and gradua-

tion are tied to performance on standardized tests. Discipline policies are severe and lead to many suspensions and some expulsions.

(3) "Cost effectiveness" is primary, placing a higher priority on saving money than providing comfort, beauty, safety, or equity. Special programs are often cut due to budgetary considerations, in spite of the need for them or their effectiveness.

(4) "Technology" is supreme, using automation to the point of excluding the human element. Teachers become as reliant on films, videos, and software packages, as they were on textbooks. The students become captives of technology.

(5) "Centralized control" reigns supreme, mandating and regulating instruction from a distance, without regard for individual differences. Power is concentrated in the hands of a few and flows from the top down. Decision making is not shared.

(6) "Workers as functionaries," in that teachers and students are expected to be passive, hardworking, and responsive to the needs of the school system without reciprocation. There is manipulation of the educative experience through external policies, programs, practices, and people.

The prevalence of these efficient factory school attributes leads to environments that breed distrust, disrespect, pessimism, and negative intentionality. They establish relationships, that are lethal and annihilate any hope of success.

Schools, like families, can be functional or dysfunctional. Functionality can be determined by applying the four levels of invitational development (Purkey, 1978; Purkey & Novak, 1984; Purkey & Schmidt, 1987) to their programs, policies, places, processes, and people. The four levels of development are:

Level One—**Intentionally Disinviting**, characterized by consistently negative messages that demean, discourage, defeat, discriminate, and/or cause disharmony with purpose. Example: (Process) A placement process, such as tracking, that is done for the purpose of segregating protected class individuals within educational programs; Level Two—**Unintentionally Disinviting**, characterized by insensitive and inconsistent negative messages that demoralize, depersonalize, and/or dehumanize without malice. Example: (Policy) A unilateral grading policy that does not allow students or teachers any flexibility. Teachers are not allowed to make exceptions based on special circumstances; Level Three—**Unintentionally Inviting**, characterized by inconsistent, yet positive, messages that engage, assuage, and encourage without direction or purpose. Example: (People) A secretary who is generally polite to every caller, but is unaware of the need to do so, and therefore discontinues the politeness under adversity; and Level Four—**Intentionally Inviting**, characterized by consistent and positive messages that celebrate, elevate, translate, and integrate with clear purpose. Example: (Program) A program designed to help bilingual students assimilate into the school's culture, which respects the students' culture, while transmitting the school's culture.

Invitational Curriculum

The curriculum that comprises the various academic and social programs promoted by a school operating under this philosophy would have to incorporate an affective component. Various levels of affective experiences would be incorporated based on the particular needs of the program or school.

Affective curriculum development (Beane, 1991) has followed three paths. First, the Personal Development Activities Approach, which focused on getting students to like themselves, through small group discussions with the teacher for specific amounts of time at a designated time. Concepts like self-love and concern for others provided the substance of these discussions. This method was followed by the Self-Esteem Courses or Programs Approach, which focused on students perceiving themselves in positive ways and behaving accordingly. These courses and programs were administered as a regular part of the school day, but adjunct to the regular curriculum, and guaranteed improved self-esteem when properly presented. The Comprehensive School Approach replaced the courses and programs approach and focused on enhancing self-esteem of all parties in the entire school, through substantially changing the substance of its policies, programs, and processes. Curriculum here includes learning experiences which are explicit, implicit, and hidden.

The invitational approach to curriculum is most compatible with the third and most recent approach, especially in its acknowledgment that the total school environment either enhances or debilitates self-esteem. Some curricular theorists suggest that all of what students experience in the school environment becomes a part of curriculum. This would include hall and cafeteria experiences.

The invitational curriculum does not consist of a set body of knowledge nor is it a series of activities, but it is a comprehensive approach to content and delivery that can be characterized as collaboratively-planned, thematically-organized, and globally-oriented. The content is free of racial, cultural, and gender bias, promotes both collective and personal efficacy, and embodies democratic principles. The emphasis is on both personal and social meaning. Proponents of invitational education believe that it is not enough to change people, but policies, processes, and programs must also change. Curriculum is one aspect of programs that must be addressed. If invitational education is to permeate a school environment, it must be an integral part of the curriculum, in both substance and form.

Invitational Teaching and Learning

Teaching

In discussing educational philosophy, one cannot ignore the centrality of the learning process. An analysis of the roles of teachers and students reveals how the process of being educated unfolds in the classroom. It alerts us to the pivotal role teachers play and the skills they must employ to accomplish the philosophical goals of schools.

Teachers and the relationships they establish with their students, through specific behaviors and comments, were the focus of the original work on invitational education (Purkey, 1978), where seven skills characterized the inviting teacher. They include reaching each student, listening with care, being real with oneself, being real with students, inviting good discipline, handling rejection, and inviting oneself. Later, Purkey and Novak (1984) expanded the theory to include an inviting process that teachers could follow to improve the self-concepts of their students. The more specific skills were subsumed under three general classifications: being ready, being with, and following through. Also, attention was given to the teacher as a total being with needs in both personal and professional areas. It was suggested that teachers should know and practice how to be inviting to themselves and others in personal and professional ways; develop an inviting "stance" rooted in optimism, respect, trust, and intentionality; and reflect on both the means they employ in their classrooms and the ends they serve.

Wilson (1986) stated that the teacher is the primary actor in the creation of an inviting classroom, establishing a warm accepting environment through invitations that are modeled, extended, and received. He characterized the inviting teacher as one who: is genuinely sincere about helping students succeed; knows the power of both invitations and disinvitations; is committed to maximizing students' development emotionally, academically, spiritually, and physically; is willing to risk inviting and being rejected, understanding that rejection of the invitation is separate from rejection of the inviter; and views invitations as classic vehicles for encouraging student growth and development.

Reed (1991) suggested that a significant part of invitational teaching is creating an environment which enhances self-esteem development by providing: a sense of uniqueness, where teachers respond to individuals rather than to labels or stereotypes; a sense of models, where teachers model the principles and behaviors they teach and expect of their students; a sense of connectiveness, where teachers make deliberate attempts to relate learning to life outside the classroom; and a sense of power, where students share the power with teachers. Beane and Lipka (1986) described the self-esteem enhancing dimension of teaching as including the ability to "help clarify values or value indicators, encourage the development of values, promote the process of valuing, help individuals examine the sources of and influences on personal values or value indicators, and encourage individuals to 'think' and improve thinking skills" (p. 9).

Schmidt (1991), in discussing "intentionality," characterized intentional inviters as people who are optimistic, respectful, empathetic, flexible, humorous, purposeful, responsible, accepting, process-oriented, and group-oriented. These qualities are not only appropriate for teachers, but are necessary. Wilson (1986) noted that intentionally-inviting teachers are: skillful and fluent in sending positive messages and signals, responsive to students' non-verbal communication, exhibit sensitivity and enthusiasm, skilled in preventing disharmony, and skilled appraisers of interactions and situations. Teachers in this mold exhibit a full-time commitment to being a beneficial presence in the lives of children, promoting their total development.

Learning

This is a student-centered view which seeks to actively engage students in self-discovery and fulfillment while helping them to understand and positively relate to others around them. The long range goal is to develop healthy, happy, competent human beings who can actively participate in our democratic society. More immediately, teachers strive to get students to actively and successfully participate in the learning process. In the invitational framework, students are invited to develop a positive view of themselves and others, to respect individual uniqueness, and to exhibit self-confidence and self-motivation. They are expected to recognize and respond to appropriate invitations, as well as to extend invitations to both themselves and others. They are believed to be capable of demonstrating self-worth and self-discipline, respecting the educative process, valuing and practicing cooperation and collaboration, and performing according to their potential. They are given opportunities to share the responsibility of creating and maintaining a positive and productive learning environment, engaging in peer tutoring, and participating in decision-making related to curriculum, instruction, discipline, and evaluation, including evaluating their own progress.

Invitational Methods and Evaluation

Methods

As with any philosophy, the methods and evaluation should be consistent with the overall purpose. In this case, the primary purpose is to increase school success. Therefore, teachers using this approach must employ diverse methods that will allow them to enhance self-concept and improve relationships.

To provide a sense of uniqueness, teachers should individualize instruction to guarantee students an opportunity to perform according to their own potential, vary teaching to accommodate different learning styles, design assignments that incorporate hemispheric strengths, multiple intelligences, and existing knowledge bases to instill confidence, and direct motivation. They also should conduct discussions to discover values and value indicators, and employ journal writing to help students express their feelings about self and others.

To provide a sense of models, they can engage cooperative and collaborative instruction to diminish competition and develop cooperative spirit. Teachers should intentionally use democratic procedures and practices to develop social competence, assigning projects and reports to develop both cognitive and affective skills, particularly valuing, analysis, responding, and evaluation. In addition, they should periodically conduct simulations and role-plays to teach responsibility.

To provide a sense of power and teach self-control, a problem-solving approach can be implemented. Teachers should plan field trips using the students' ideas and suggestions for place and purpose. Self-efficacy and collective efficacy can be encouraged through peer tutoring and peer teaching. Teachers should use accelerated instruction instead of remediation to promote interest and self-confidence.

To promote a sense of connectiveness, teachers can integrate students' life experiences into classroom learning. They can use creative dramatics, art, and music to reveal students' needs, interests, and hidden talents. Inclusion of materials which reflect the make-up of the class would be essential.

If the purpose of education is to improve relationships and invite success, then teachers must strive for maximum competency instead of minimal competency. Based on their knowledge of their students, teachers must send invitations that confirm the capability, responsibility, and value of their students (Reed, 1991; Beane, 1991; Wilson, 1986; Lewis & Purkey, 1983).

Evaluation

Student Evaluation--Just as inviting teachers are encouraged to use varied methods of teaching, they are also expected to diversify evaluation strategies. Some recommended strategies include using teacher assessments which are objective and subjective, graded and non-graded, criterion-referenced, free of racial, cultural, or gender bias; using some assessments which are co-designed; making criterion clear to students before each assessment; conferencing with students after assessments; using measures that determine both what students know and are able to do as a result of the knowledge; using measures that determine affective growth and development (i.e., motivation, self-perception, locus of control, etc.); testing only what has been assigned, taught, or reviewed; using class observations and interviews to determine growth and development in the area of social interaction skills; using wholistic grading to evaluate writing and speaking skills, if grading is necessary; and using peer and self-evaluation frequently.

Teacher Evaluation--Since the teacher is such an important force in the invitational model, teacher evaluation is essential. Teachers need to know: if they are successful in being an inviting person and professional; if they are demonstrating skills in a fluent or artful manner; if their stance demonstrates optimism, trust, respect, and intentionality; and if the relationships they form with students are beneficial. They can find this out by seeking student input through formal surveys, informal rap sessions, class meetings, class activities, and a suggestion box; seeking peer input through class observations, videotape reviews, and informal conversations; seeking principal or supervisor input through class observations, effective and inviting behavioral scales, videotape reviews, and student interviews; seeking parent input through brief surveys, conferences, class observations, a suggestion box, or informal conversations; and self-assessing by observing their interactions with other students, being aware of their comments and behaviors, observing student response to their invitations, keeping a record of the number, type, and frequency of their invitations, perhaps noting the recipient in each case (Reed, 1991; Beane, 1991; Wilson, 1986). Through these different measures, both students and teachers can know their progress in the process and make changes as needed.

What is Multicultural Education?

Multicultural education (Gollnick & Chinn, 1986) is a theory of practice designed to assist all students in realizing their potential for academic, vocational, and social success, through valuing cultural diversity, portraying various cultural backgrounds positively, and using cultural diversity in the development of effective instructional strategies. Banks (1987) suggested that a major goal is to change the entire educational environment to one which is respectful of cultural diversity and enables students of all cultural groups to have an equal educational opportunity. Gollnick and Chinn (1986) offered a parallel goal, which is to help students overcome the pervasive and deleterious effects of institutionalized racism, as well as classism and sexism.

Multicultural education, according to George N. Wallace (Sims & Bass de Martinez, 1981) "is simply good, diagnostic, and prescriptive or individualized teaching" (p. 89), where teachers find out about each of their students' backgrounds academically and culturally, their level of development, their values, interests, and significant relationships.

Leicester (1989) explicated three interpretations of multicultural education by placing initial emphasis on the multicultural aspect.

They are: education **through** many cultures—where multicultural elements are utilized to deliver instruction and facilitate integration; education **in** many cultures—where various cultural traditions are presented as paradigms in the educative process to foster pluralism; and education **for** a multicultural society—where moral imperatives, such as justice, equality, and freedom, are taught explicitly to eliminate racism. Each interpretation clearly leads to a different type of education, while the term remains the same.

Assumptions

Proponents of multicultural education believe that respect for diversity and individual uniqueness is essential to life in a multicultural, anti-racist society. Some common underlying assumptions of this theory of practice, identified by Tiedt and Tiedt (1990), include:

1. Every aspect of life is multicultural, since our society is multicultural;

2. Multicultural education begins with self-esteem for each person;

3. Labeling can be dangerous when it is not used sensitively and respectfully;

4. Children grow up in particular cultures and enter schools with a wealth of prior knowledge drawn from their cultural experiences;

5. Multicultural education deals with personal and sensitive issues, such as attitudes and values, which involve students directly in their learning;

6. Students and teachers can be made aware of their own thinking and that of others within a multicultural framework;

7. Students can develop the ability to make sound decisions and appropriate choices using this framework; and

8. Approaching education multiculturally develops understanding and acceptance of racial, cultural, and ethnic diversity. (p. 326-327)

This philosophical approach, according to Tiedt & Tiedt (1990), contradicts the traditional perspective of the monocultural "melting pot" metaphor, which suggests that the dominant culture is superior to other cultures and therefore should subsume those subordinate cultures completely. Instead, they suggested that a "tossed salad" metaphor more ideally represents the desirable status of culture in America, where distinct cultures co-exist within the dominant culture, enriching and strengthening it, while maintaining their unique characteristics and integrity.

The "tossed salad" metaphor implies that each component culture has inherent integrity and brings something special and unique to the overall recipe. Diversity is seen as a positive ingredient, rather than an imperfection, disadvantage, or deficiency. This view leads to the enhancement of ethnic identity and positive self-esteem, as well as a respect for and an understanding of the ethnic heritage of others. Conversely, implicit in the "melting pot" metaphor is a lack of respect for cultural and ethnic diversity, which leads to a lack of ethnic pride and low self-esteem. This is especially true when indigenous language, customs, values, and other artifacts of culture are devalued and subordinated during the process of blending into the dominant culture (Reed, 1991).

Another metaphor, offered by Robert Thompson (Reed, 1989), describes America's diversity as a cultural "bouillabaisse," a hearty stew. America's "bouillabaisse" quality is not only in its diversity, but also in how that diversity is shaped and changed in the various societal processes, where some ingredients—cultures— remain more intact, while others dissipate. His metaphor implies that while each culture offers something unique to the national recipe, some contributions are more visible than others, though they may not be more substantial. This median metaphor seems to address our present status on the multicultural continuum.

There is strong evidence that by accepting the "melting pot" metaphor, schools have institutionalized both beliefs and practices which undermine positive cultural identity and feelings of efficacy, as well as perpetuate discriminatory treatment.

Sims (1981) identified three seminal ideas of Western European origin, embedded in the American ethos, which have had a great impact on education in America:

1) a perception of the culturally and racially different as inferior;

2) an intense emphasis on respect for authority, obedience to family, and loyalty to God; and

3) a disposition to regard anything short of perfection as unacceptable... (p. 2).

He argued that the most damaging part of the American ethos has been its embracement of racial and cultural inferiority, which has led to discriminatory practices both in and out of schools. He specifically criticized the discriminatory testing and placement practices of schools in the case of the culturally different student. Hilliard (1990) emphatically stated that schools have scandalously and disproportionately placed students of racially, linguistically, and economically different backgrounds in special education, have held lower expectations of them, and have suspended and expelled them more often, all due to institutionalized racism.

The Shipman study reviewed by Tiedt and Tiedt (1990) revealed that children enter school with essentially the same average level of self-esteem, but after only three years of schooling, clear differences exist for low- and middle-class students. Low-income students, who are disproportionately ethnically- and racially-identifiable, are adversely affected by the schooling experience, as evidenced by lower self-esteem and self-confidence.

Pine and Hilliard (1990) agreed that racism, prejudice, and discriminatory practices are sabotaging America's efforts to provide a quality education for all students. They argued that in spite of the attention and lip service given to educational equity, culturally different students still have to contend with both overt and insidious forms of racism which thwart their aspirations and undermine their self-confidence. Another tragedy in this sad scenario is the damage done to the children holding these distorted views of themselves as being superior to the culturally different. In order to combat the devastating effects of this monocultural approach on all students, they suggested: the development and implementation of a multicultural curriculum; the perfecting of pedagogical practices; hiring more teachers from communities of color; intentionally confronting and challenging racism; enhancing student self-esteem; and teaching character development.

Given the previously stated assumptions, beliefs, and goals of multicultural education, a particular orientation to curriculum, teaching and learning, methods, and evaluation emerges and supports the multicultural framework.

Multicultural Curriculum

There are several approaches to multicultural curriculum development. Banks (1988) described a hierarchy of four approaches which identified levels of integration of ethnic content. They are:

Level One—**The Contributions Approach**, characterized by a focus on integrating heroes and heroines, holidays, and discrete elements of culture into the monocultural curriculum, without changing the basic structure, goals, or fundamental characteristics of the existing curriculum. Example: The celebration of Mexican Independence Day with emphasis on Mexican heroes and heroines;

Level Two—**The Ethnic Additive Approach**, characterized by a focus on supplementing the regular curriculum with ethnic themes, concepts, content, and perspectives, without changing the basic struc-

ture, goals, or fundamental characteristics. Example: The addition of the *Autobiography of Malcolm
X* to a Eurocentric literature class syllabus;
Level Three—**The Transformation Approach,**
characterized by an infusion of other ethnic content and perspectives which change the structure
of the curriculum and its underlying assumptions,
enabling students to engage concepts, issues,
themes, and dilemmas from several perspectives
and viewpoints. Example: Custer's last stand presented from the Sioux Nation's perspective, pre-
ceded by a sensitive treatment of how the Sioux
Nation viewed the changes occurring around them
at the time; and
Level Four—**The Decision-Making and Social
Action Approach,** characterized by the infused
curriculum and other features noted in the Transformation Approach, enhanced by students engaging in decision-making and action-taking related to solving social problems. Example: Students tackle the issue of racism in their school.

Banks concluded that when multicultural curriculum is developed and implemented at level four, students learn thinking skills
and decision-making skills, as well as a sense of efficacy.

When the curriculum is viewed as a series of multicultural
concepts, topics, and competencies that are woven throughout the
K-12 program, rather than added on to it, students become truly
culturally literate and sensitive (Tiedt & Tiedt, 1990). They learn
the complete story of history, are exposed to art and music from
around the world, read literature that truly represents a global
perspective, learn foreign language in the context of the culture,
study the relatedness of their environment to other environments,
and essentially learn a non-western story of the world (Reed, 1991;
Reed, 1990; Pine & Hilliard, 1990). If the curriculum begins with

self-esteem as a bottom line and spirals upward toward the ultimate goal of world peace, as suggested by Tiedt and Tiedt (1990), students will become aware of their own ethnic, cultural, and racial backgrounds, beliefs and attitudes, and personal habits and behaviors, as well as those of others.

Multicultural Teaching and Learning

Teaching

Diversity is present in urban, rural, and suburban districts, even when that diversity is not very visible. Very few, if any, American public schools have a truly monocultural population. A surface analysis will reveal religious, cultural, linguistic, and economic diversity in most settings. Therefore, teachers must be aware of and sensitive to the various challenges that face students in their homes and communities as they prepare for the teaching-learning process. Knapp and Shields (1990) suggested that educational effectiveness could improve if teachers of the culturally diverse were aware that: focusing on student deficits can lead to inaccurate assessments of children's strengths and weaknesses; faulty and inappropriate low expectations are extracted from the deficit view of students; focusing on deficits draws disproportionate attention to what students **cannot** do; and focusing on family dysfunction makes it nearly impossible to see students' potential for success and the strengths they could apply to achieve that success. They further contend that teachers need to begin with the assumption "that all students arrive at school with ways of speaking and interacting with adults and peers and with ideas about the purpose of schooling and the likelihood of their success" (p. 755).

In describing what should be done to improve efficacy with multicultural populations, they suggested that teachers provide numerous opportunities for teacher/student and student/student discussions, use heterogeneous groups, teach strategies that allow students to self monitor, problem solve, and follow through on assignments independently, use supplemental instruction in a flexible and integrated manner, and be flexible about classroom decorum, allowing for environmental and structural changes to accommodate the diversity of class activities.

Recognizing that the teacher's role is primary in the educative process, and particularly so in the case of diverse populations, teachers in this framework respect students by selecting and employing methods that accommodate cultural and individual differences, integrating ethnic content and varying perspectives into the curriculum to promote a more global view, and using multiple sources of evaluation that yield quantitative and qualitative measures of student performance. They believe all students can learn and hold appropriate expectations of all students, thereby providing learning opportunities that develop higher order skills, as well as reinforce basic skills, and model good communication and social interaction skills. These teachers are aware of and use various motivational techniques while facilitating the learning process, locating both internal and external resources. They seek to establish links among the family, school, and community at large. Finally, they seek to manage the class through democratic principles instead of authoritarian rule, and encourage cooperation and collaboration among students instead of competition (Reed, 1990, 1991; Tiedt & Tiedt, 1990; Pine & Hilliard, 1990).

Learning

The multicultural view of learning is student-centered, engaging the student directly and actively in the learning process. The student is expected to be self-motivated, develop and use inquiry skills, develop and use discovery skills, question established practices, demonstrate responsible decision-making skills, demonstrate social interaction skills, and become an agent for change in the classroom, school, community, and, eventually, the society.

Also, students are expected to analyze and synthesize ideas and concepts, as well as evaluate practices and assumptions. They are expected to demonstrate valuing as it relates to beliefs, cultural customs, and practices, and organize values and determine their interrelatedness, as well as make generalizations pertaining to values, ultimately integrating them into a personal philosophy of life.

Multicultural Methods and Evaluation

Methods

Since the multicultural approach focuses primarily on personal goals, such as the development of self-esteem and positive cultural identity, and secondarily on societal goals, such as developing empathy and respect for others and reducing racial prejudice, it is imperative that the methods of instruction be diverse. They should include, but not be limited to: individualized instruction to meet the diverse needs of students; cooperative learning to increase collaboration and sharing and de-emphasize competition; projects and reports to encourage social awareness and sensitivity; simulations and role-plays to develop empathy and respect for differences; guest speakers and trips to expose students to the ethnic, economic, linguistic, religious, and racial diversity of their community resources; discussions to share various perspectives; multiple stimuli, such as computers, videos, and audio-tapes, to reinforce learning through engaging multiple senses simultaneously; the arts as a universal language and a symbol of commonality, to build self-esteem and reduce racism; experimentation to test established political, social, economic, legal, medical, and educational practices and assumptions; problem solving to encourage social activism; and brainstorming to generate collective solutions to problems (Reed, 1991; Tiedt & Tiedt, 1990; Bondi & Wiles, 1989).

Evaluation

Evaluation should measure the degree to which identified goals and objectives are met and the processes used in attaining those objectives. Multicultural teaching stresses both cognitive and affective outcomes; therefore, both types of measures should be used. Multiple approaches to assessment should be used to yield both quantitative and qualitative data about student progress and achievement. Other factors that will influence evaluation are the degree to which learning is individualized, open-ended, experiential, experimental, and/or integrated.

Bondi and Wiles (1989) illustrated both Bloom's taxonomy of educational objectives from the cognitive domain and Krathwohl's taxonomy of the affective domain, showing the interrelatedness of the various skill levels. The cognitive domain includes knowledge, comprehension, application, analysis, synthesis, and evaluation. The affective domain includes receiving, responding, valuing, organization, and characterization. The multicultural outcomes identified by Tiedt and Tiedt (1990) focus on the development of the full range of cognitive and affective skills, not just the lower level skills. With this broad range of desired outcomes, it is imperative to employ creative and diversified evaluative measures.

Some suggested guidelines in planning for multicultural evaluation are: to only grade selected student work and never grade a first draft of a student's writing, allowing students to revise their work as much as possible; always make the grading criteria clear for the grades you give, sharing samples of work at each level; encourage self-assessment by requiring that students check their own work often and by supplying answer sheets when appropriate; have brief weekly conferences with each student, if possible, discussing progress honestly and actively listening; conduct paper dialogues with students when individual conferences are impossible, writing notes on returned assignments, on separate note cards, or in journals; allow multiple performances where possible, as well as alternative methods. If the important thing is that students acquire certain knowledge, skills, and abilities, then how and when they demonstrate them should be negotiable; send a letter of commendation to parents several times during the year to make them aware of their child's accomplishments. If you are dealing with a bilingual home, provide a translation of the letter as a courtesy; accentuate the positive as often as possible, but keep the praise genuine and appropriate. In most cases, empty praise is as painful as no praise. In addition, you should test what you teach, assign, or know students have learned; otherwise, the evaluation is unfair. Evaluation, like discipline, is necessary, but must be fair (Tiedt & Tiedt, 1990; Reed, 1991).

Compatibility of Invitational and Multicultural Education

These two philosophical approaches, invitational and multicultural, have much in common from their purposes to appropriate evaluation measures. The invitational literature specifically mentions multicultural aspects, while the multicultural literature makes several references to affective aspects of education, which invitational education promotes. The charts on pages 70 and 71 show specific areas of similarity and compatibility.

Implications

All schools can profit from both invitational education and multicultural education. What is needed is a belief that all children can learn and a desire on the part of educators to offer the best opportunity for all students to learn. We can no longer afford to ignore differences, promote homogeneity, or relegate culturally different or poor students to marginal status. Doing a better job of educating all the children is in the best interest of the entire society, especially as it relates to the financial and social costs of future unemployment, welfare, medical care, and incarceration.

Invitational education offers a well-developed plan to teachers and other helpers in the school for communicating and behaving in ways that invite positive self-concept, self-esteem, and educational success. It gives educational leaders a framework upon which to draw when developing policies and programs, designing places, assigning people, and formulating processes. Multicultural education provides both substance and form for the curriculum, as well as a framework for educators to acquire and model sensitivity and respect for diversity.

Both educational approaches help define the role of teacher and student in a humane and productive way that moves away from teacher as authoritarian and student as passive vessel waiting to be filled. They also provide a more positive lens from which to view student potential, skills, and abilities, as well as eliminating the need to perceive students in terms of deficits and disadvantages. Instead, teachers can celebrate the diversity, uniqueness, and limitless potential of their students and themselves.

Each approach delineates methods which consider the needs of the students over the convenience of educators. Neither invitational nor multicultural education condones methods which ignore diversity or individuality, and they complement each other on issues of evaluation by avoiding bias, uniformity, and unnecessary competition. Clearly, these theories of practice have much in common and should be intentionally comingled and applied in the educative process for the benefit of all.

Invitational education and multicultural education are not panaceas, but they offer educators an opportunity to right some wrongs and prevent further damage to the self-esteem of thousands of students who are disinvited and made marginal or invisible in schools. These schools disinvite by acting as if they were monocultural institutions, ignoring their true diversity.

AREAS OF COMPATIBILITY

Invitational Education *(Individual)*	*Multicultural Education* *(Individual and Societal)*

Goals

1. To invite academic success.

1. To promote academic, vocational, and social success.

2. To enhance self-concept and self-esteem.

2. To promote positive self-esteem, especially related to culture.

3. To create more loving, accepting and friendly schools.

3. To create more culturally sensitive schools.

4. To direct student motivation toward positive outcomes.

4. To develop intrinsic motivation through extrinsic motivational strategies.

5. To change policies, places, programs, processes, and people.

5. To re-think policies and procedures that have a discriminatory effect.

Curriculum

1. Ideally is a comprehensive approach to education that permeates every aspect of schooling.

1. Ideally, multicultural content is woven throughout the entire curriculum, changing its structure and underlying assumptions.

2. Is much more than a particular program or course.

2. Is more than a course, program of study, or special activity.

Teaching

1. Teachers are primary actors in the educative process.

1. Teachers are pivotal in the educative process.

2. Teachers facilitate student learning.

2. Teachers facilitate learning by locating internal and external resources.

3. Teachers model inviting skills personally and professionally.

3. Teachers model good social interaction and communication skills.

AREAS OF COMPATIBILITY (continued)

Invitational Education *(Individual)*	*Multicultural Education* *(Individual and Societal)*

Learning

1. Students learn to be self-motivated and self-disciplined.

2. Students see themselves and others as individuals with unique personalities.

1. Students learn to be self-motivated and to use inquiry, decision-making, and social interaction skills.

2. Students see each other as members of ethnic, cultural, or racial groups, with unique personal styles, beliefs and behaviors.

Methods

1. Requires multiple methods.
2. Individualizing and cooperative learning are essential.

1. Requires diverse methods.
2. Cooperative and experiential learning are essential.

Evaluation

1. Utilizes objective and subjective measures.
2. Utilizes teacher, peer and self assessment.
3. Includes individual conferences, observations, and positive feedback.

1. Utilizes quantitative and qualitative data.
2. Utilizes teacher and self assessment.
3. Includes written feedback and weekly conferences.

As educators ponder restructuring, they should carefully consider the boon of these approaches, for it would be a shame to restructure racism, making it less visible, but just as lethal, or to restructure classism so programs take on new euphemisms but maintain their tracking and sorting functions. Restructuring, from an invitational and multicultural perspective, requires more than renaming a school, planting bushes, naming parents to advisory councils, talking about empowerment, or having some fiscal control. It requires: a change of perspective on culture and race, from a monolithic white majority group that is perceived to be monocultural and superior, to a multicultural perception that is inclusive of all other racial or cultural groups as equals; a change of perception about student efficacy and worth, from disabled and worthless to enabled and valued; a change of stance on teacher efficacy, from pessimistic and overwhelmed to optimistic and responsible; and finally, a change of behavior in relation to self and others, from disinviting and sometimes lethal interactions to inviting and consistently beneficial interactions.

Conclusion

Proponents of multicultural education have made their stand on self-esteem issues very clear. It is time for the proponents of invitational education to make emphatic their support of diversity and equity. This can be done, as Novak (1986) suggested, by extending the theory to go beyond the surface and to deal with the difficult and deep questions of racism, sexism, and classism and their relationship to the educative process. This chapter has already established the compatibility of the invitational approach with multicultural education, which specifically addresses these concerns. What is needed now is intentional action on the part of invitational theorists to examine questions posed by Novak (1986) that explore all the possible relationships between and among students, teachers, curriculum, governance, and the social world.

If the purpose of a philosophy is to provide a fundamental framework through which all educational processes can best be understood, then invitational education as a theory of practice must extend itself to examine: (a) the nature and source of the values upon which it is based, (b) the type of education and subject matter it endorses, (c) the resulting teaching and learning process, and, ultimately, (d) the system of evaluation that best measures its effectiveness, as related to the challenges of educating diverse populations.

The risk for invitational education is to lose being viewed as "that wonderful non-threatening feel-good approach to education;" however the need for change is greater than the risk. Too many children are being disinvited, disowned, and/or discouraged, and as a result, "diseducated." They struggle through irrelevant educational programs, delivered by too many insensitive and misinformed teachers, who follow policies and procedures that often contradict an inviting and multicultural stance on education. If these students graduate, their diplomas are virtually meaningless, because of the low performance that is expected and accepted. These students need every individual associated with the learning process to be an advocate. The challenge is to make every person in the educational setting accountable for his or her words and deeds in the creation of an inviting multicultural environment.

This challenge will allow invitational educators to shape significant changes in both the structure and delivery systems of schools, to benefit children who are culturally, economically, linguistically, and racially different or otherwise disinvited, without hampering or otherwise hurting the success of other students.

References

Banks, J. A. (1988). Approaches to multicultural reform. *Multicultural Leader*, Winter, 1-2.

Banks, J. A. (1987). *Teaching strategies for ethnic studies* (4th edition). Boston, MA: Allyn & Bacon.

Beane, J. A. (1991). Sorting out the self-esteem controversy. *Educational Leadership, 49*(1), 25-30.

Beane, J. A., & Lipka, R. P. (1986). *Self-esteem, self-concept, and the curriculum* (1st edition). New York: Teachers College Press.

Gollnick, D. M., & Chinn, P. C. (1986). *Multicultural education in a pluralistic society* (2nd edition). Columbus, OH: Merrill.

Hilliard III, A. G. (1991). Do we have the will to educate all poor children? *Educational Leadership, 49*(1), 31-36.

Hilliard III, A. G. (1989). Teachers and cultural styles in a pluralistic society. *National Education Association Today, 7*(6), 65-69.

Knapp, M. S., & Shields, P. M. (1990) Reconceiving academic instruction for the children of poverty. *Phi Delta Kappan, 71*(10), 752-758.

Lambeth, C. R. (1980). Teacher invitations and effectiveness as reported by students in a Virginia high school. Unpublished doctoral dissertation, University of Virginia.

Leicester, M. (1989). *Multicultural education: Theory to practice* (1st edition). Windsor, England: NFER-NELSON.

Lewis, H. G., & Purkey, W. W. (1983). Efficient factory or inviting family? Two school models for the 21st century. *Journal of Humanistic Education, 21*(7), 31-33.

Novak, J. M. (1989; April). Toward an integrated theory of inviting: Skills, craft, and art. Paper presented at the American Educational Research Association Annual Meeting, San Francisco, CA.

Pine, G. J., & Hilliard, III, A. G. (1990) Rx for racism: Imperatives for America's schools. *Phi Delta Kappan, 71*(8), 593-600.

Purkey, W. W. (1978). *Inviting school success: A self-concept approach to teaching and learning* (1st edition). Belmont, CA: Wadsworth.

Purkey, W. W., & Novak, J. M. (1984). *Inviting school success: A self-concept approach to teaching and learning* (2nd edition). Belmont, CA: Wadsworth.

Purkey, W. W., & Schmidt, J. J. (1987) *The inviting relationship: An expanded perspective for professional helping.* Englewood Cliffs, NJ: Prentice-Hall.

Reed, C. (1991, May). Can culture empower? Presentation at the National Alliance of Black School Educator's Regional Meeting, Milwaukee, WI.

Reed, C. (1989, November). Self-concept: A cultural context. Speech presented at the Metropolitan Milwaukee Alliance of Black School Educator's Annual Meeting, Milwaukee, WI.

Reed, C. (1984, April). Black self-concept and achievement. Paper presented at the American Educational Research Association Annual Meeting, New Orleans, LA.

Reed, I. (1989). What's American about America toward claiming our multicultural heritage. *Utne Reader*, March/April, 100-105.

Sims, W. E., & Bass de Martinez, B. (1981). *Perspectives in Multicultural Education* (1st edition). Lanham, MD: University Press.

Tiedt, P. L., and Tiedt, I. M. (1990). *Multicultural teaching: A handbook of activities, information and resources* (3rd. edition). Needham Heights, MA: Allyn & Bacon.

Wilson, J. H. (1986). *Invitational elementary classroom* (1st edition). Springfield, IL: Charles C Thomas.

Wiles, J. E., & Bondi, J. (1989). *Curriculum Development: A guide to practice* (3rd edition). Columbus, OH: Merrill.

Chapter 5
Invitational Theory: Applications in Physical Education

By John Kearns

Physical Education! Phys. Ed.! Fizz Ed! No matter what you call it, or what one's memories of this curriculum area are, the feelings are seldom if ever neutral. For many students the memories are of excitement, competition, fun, and success. For increasing numbers of students, however, physical education is remembered as a time to stand in line, a time to be ignored because the teacher spent most of the time with the "jocks," or a time to publicly display one's incompetence and be publicly embarrassed and humiliated. Two very extreme sets of feelings, really. But the situation that is remembered by most students when they reflect on their years in "fizz ed" often line up behind one of these two poles.

The purpose of this chapter will be to examine the state of physical education in light of invitational theory.

Physical Education Today

If one thinks about what physical education should be, the idea of playing games would probably come quickly to mind. One would think, too, that children want to have fun. Therefore, physical education should be in most cases the favorite curriculum area for students. It seems logical enough on the surface, but underlying this attempt for adults to understand the thinking of children is the sorry truth. While fun and games are appealing to children, two out of three students in Canada choose not to enroll in a physical education class after the mandatory credit in grade nine (Sawchuk, 1989). Many would drop physical education from their selection of courses much earlier if the option was available to them.

Why? Clearly, they are not having fun! Their needs are not being met! How disinviting! When students have the option to select courses, in increasing numbers they choose not to select physical education. Despite strong encouragement and endorsement from the American and Canadian Medical Associations, insurance companies, and government, students are turning away from physical education. Despite recent trends in personal fitness becoming more prominent in North American society in the past two decades, when students have the option to opt out, they do! Why?

What are the needs and expectations of children with regard to sports and physical education classes?

Identified Needs of Children in Physical Education

Many studies (Alderman, 1976; Birch & Veroff, 1966; Straub, 1980) have found that children are basically motivated by the same incentives with regard to physical activity. When surveyed, children have identified seven incentive conditions that meet their needs. They are: independence, power, affiliation, excellence, aggression, stress, and success.

Independence

Many children find themselves in situations in the classroom where their every move is seemingly monitored. They are instructed to line up when the bell goes, ask for permission to leave the room, complete assignment A before proceeding to assignment B, and so on. Other children come from homes which are constraining and over-protective.

In sport, children find that there is often an opportunity to do things without the help and interference from others. So, for many children, the opportunity to engage in a sporting activity meets their needs in terms of acting independently from others, especially adults.

Power

Power incentives are those in which a student has the opportunity to influence and control other people. There is the opportunity to influence their attitudes, interests, and opinions. This incentive is interesting because its strength is situation specific.

For instance, imagine a student who is struggling academically. For this individual to make a suggestion in the context of a reading class, part of the power of the suggestion would be cloaked in the perception that the other members of the class have of that student within that context. In this case, the class members would see a non-academic student trying to assert influence and would judge that suggestion partially with the social position of the student in mind.

Now take the same student, who is an athletic leader, and put him or her into a soccer situation. Making a suggestion to the group in this context will give the student and suggestion more credibility. The suggestion comes from a situational leader and deserves, and will likely be given, appropriate consideration. This incentive condition meets the needs of some students in a physical education environment.

Affiliation

Affiliation needs are those that revolve around opportunities for social interaction, or being socially accepted and providing evidence that one is worthwhile by making friends or by maintaining friendships that are already established.

We have all seen commercials that depict people playing "ol' timer" ball or hockey. The commercial inevitably concludes with the players enjoying some social time together...the company of good friends. While this scenario is true of adults in sport, it is no less valid for children. The opportunity to build and maintain friendships is a human motivational force and a basic need. Physical education for some students provides an environment where this need can be uniquely met.

Stress

Stress, as it is typically referred to in North America, has received a lot of negative press recently. However, the definition of "stress" as it is used as a motivating factor for children in physical education means an incentive that is characterized by excitement, tension, pressure, and the pure action that a sporting context can provide. The opportunity to run, jump, and "let loose" is a prime reason that children cite when they are asked what they enjoy about physical education. In a word, "fun!"

Excellence

Excellence is defined not as doing something flawlessly, but rather as seeing oneself improve, doing something better than one has done it before. This is a sense of accomplishment that has been referred to in the literature (Kearns, 1987) as a factor in enhancing the self-esteem of an individual. Often rewards and praise are reserved for students who perform at a lofty level of attainment. While it is important to recognize superior levels of performance, most students do not function either academically or in sport at an elite level. All students can, however, perform at a personal best level of attainment. Students cite this definition of excellence as an important motivator for themselves in physical education.

Aggression

Aggression incentives are seen as opportunities to subdue, intimidate, dominate, or even injure others. Activities where aggression might be a motivating factor for involvement are hockey, football, wrestling, boxing, etc. While these sport areas do encourage aggressive behavior, and some athletes do cite aggression as a motivating factor for themselves, most participants in these and like activities do not rank aggression incentives highly when compared to other motivating incentives. A ranking of these factors will follow shortly.

Success

Success as a motivating incentive is defined as an extrinsic reward that sport can provide. Social approval, status, prestige, trophies, team jackets, etc., are symbols of success that often attract students to a sporting context. In some cases, the position that a student plays on a team (e.g., quarterback) may indicate to that student and others a level of success. Student satisfaction with physical education is closely tied to an individual's need for extrinsic indicators of success.

Interdependence of Needs

It is hypothesized that these are seven needs that students have and expect to have met in physical education and/or sporting situations. They are not necessarily independent of one another but probably amalgamate in various combinations.

Alderman and Wood (1976) have noted that enough data has been gathered regarding student needs using inventories administered to several thousand students to give some very strong indicators to coaches and physical education teachers:

> 1. The two strongest and most consistent needs for children in physical education are affiliation and excellence.
>
> 2. Stress runs a consistent third as a recognized need.
>
> 3. Children are basically motivated by the same needs regardless of their age, sex, sport, or culture.

While the research regarding student needs in physical education has been available for many years, disinviting practices continue. In one descriptive study (Anderson & Barrette, 1978), researchers noted the following patterns of behavior in physical education classes. Students spent approximately 66 percent of their time in non-movement kinds of behavior and only 36 percent of their time moving. Of this time, only 25 percent of the time was spent moving to accomplish physical education class objectives.

It was noted that 25 percent of the time was spent receiving information, and a full 66 percent of the time was spent either waiting or listening to the teacher. In contrast, only 15 percent of the time was used in practicing motor skills, 10 percent of the time game-playing, and approximately 4 percent of the time exercising. If one considers also that most physical education classes are scheduled for between 30 and 40 minutes, it is easy to see how little time is available for meeting the needs that students have in this area.

In another study (Wilcox, 1987), it was reported that many physical education teachers do not:

> 1. Plan lessons in advance;

2. Adapt lessons to the needs of individual students;

3. Provide positive reinforcement for learning;

4. Provide adequate opportunity for practice of skills;

5. Provide enough vigorous activity to contribute to fitness;

6. Prevent waste of time on managerial tasks;

7. Provide prompt and specific feedback for practice tasks; and

8. Provide clear models for desired learning.

How disinviting! To have this knowledge and yet still ignore student needs! Such practices would not be tolerated in reading or mathematics; however, physical education is typically not viewed as a serious curriculum area, despite recent societal trends in this direction.

These two studies are by no means isolated observations. The poor programs and failure to meet student needs have almost become proverbial within the physical education profession. In examining three of the main needs identified by the students— excellence, affiliation, and stress—conclusions can quickly be drawn about how disinviting practices are interpreted by students and how these practices are reflected in the dropout rates of students from this area of instruction.

According to Anderson and Barrette (1978), students spend the vast majority of the physical education time in non-physical kinds of behavior when they are in class. If one could imagine attempting to learn to ride a bicycle or learn how to swim by primarily listening to instruction, one could quickly begin to appreciate how excellence needs are not met in today's gym class.

Looking at some of the hockey greats who have developed in Canada in the past fifty years sheds some light on the need for practise time in order to meet the excellence need. Gordie Howe from Floral, Saskatchewan, spent hours practicing on a frozen slough during the winter months. Bobby Orr from Parry Sound, Ontario, practiced long hours on an outdoor rink to improve his skill level. And Wayne Gretzky's father flooded the backyard and made it into an outdoor rink so that Wayne could practice and improve his hockey skills. But what does all this have to do with physical education and students needs?

Simply this: for the most part, the only opportunity students have today to practice their sport skills are during the time provided for them by adults, be it in physical education class or during a team practice. We know too, that the time spent in physical activity designed to improve skills is nearly non-existent. If one notes the number of times that children are observed playing sports on either a ball diamond, soccer field, or outdoor rink, without the activity being organized by adults, it is easy to see that the opportunity for children to improve their sport skills is minimal. Children are rarely seen playing sports or sport-related activities on their own. The need to see progress in skill development is not being realized. What children do meet are increasing degrees of frustrations and the knowledge that their athletic dreams will not be realized.

Affiliation needs also become frustrated. Children wanting to be with their friends is natural. Many children will sign up for a sport because their friends are enrolling. In physical education classes, most students have a number of friends within their class. However, a typical teacher direction given in a gymnasium might be "Pick a partner for the next activity...." Almost inevitably, students will pick a partner who has a similar level of athletic ability to their own.

Imagine this scenario. Students are instructed to choose a partner to play catch with a soft ball. If one partner has a significantly lower level of ability than the other, throwing the ball accurately and catching the ball consistently are unlikely. The result is that the able partner does not have the ball come into his or her area often enough for it to be a satisfying experience. In addition, the able student has to wait while the unskilled partner runs after a missed ball that has not been caught. Consequently, students choose partners who are at a similar level of ability to themselves.

To extend this scenario to its logical conclusion, the able students receive significantly more successful practice than do the less skilled students. The natural gulf of development of athletic ability further separates friends and makes the likelihood of the affiliation need being met more remote. Students who have been friends prior to a sporting experience may find that their friends associate with other students in physical education. This practice is distasteful and is associated with physical education. In the eyes of many students, this is a situation worth avoiding.

Consider also the stress incentive mentioned by students as a major expectation in physical education. Students want to be part of the action. They want to have fun and "play the game." Over time, there is a positive correlation between skill level and willingness to participate in a physical activity. Those who display a personally acceptable level of expertise are more likely to want to engage further in activity, thereby becoming increasingly more able. Their need for stress is being met. Conversely, the opposite is also true. From an early age students are aware of abilities and, more to the point, their inabilities. This perception strongly influences the extent to which they are willing to publicly commit themselves to an activity. So for less able performers, their stress needs are less likely to be met because they are less likely to want to participate.

Inviting Practices and their Results

It was mentioned earlier that two out of three students in Canada no longer elect to take physical education after the mandatory grade nine credit. The dropout rate from physical education for girls is even more extreme. However, following the guidelines for inviting teaching environments and strategies provided by Purkey and Novak (1984), several secondary schools in Hamilton, Ontario, have addressed the declining enrollment of girls from physical education classes.

The results have been most encouraging. Over a four-year span, the girls' retention rate has grown to 87 percent from less than 33 percent. What this means is that of the girls who were enrolled in physical education in grade nine, 87 percent were still enrolled four years later. What is also surprising is that during the same four years, the retention rates for boys in the same system, but not following invitational practices, had not changed (Fraser, 1990).

The remainder of this chapter will outline the specific invitational focus that was adopted in the Hamilton schools to bring about this encouraging trend in women's physical education.

Variety but Simplicity in Programs

In Hamilton, physical education programs have been developed in response to both the perceived need of students and the facilities available in both the school and the local community. Every program offers a wide variety of activities. Activity units are shorter, one to two weeks, than are typically found in most secondary programs. This is a response to needs expressed by the students. Although not everyone likes each activity to the same extent, students realize that a new activity will be introduced shortly that may be more in keeping with their personal interests. Consequently, they view this format as more acceptable because they have the knowledge that the less desirable activities will be short-lived.

Students also do individual goal setting based on their current level of performance. The aim is to allow each student to see that personal performance levels increase during the classes. Students view this as personally meaningful and appropriate to their own individual needs and interests. This approach necessitates that activity levels remain high and students are involved. Be it a skill acquisition, skill development, or a game application, every attempt is made on the part of staff to ensure that students have personal success and enjoyment of the activities.

Varied Teaching Techniques

Teachers in the Hamilton schools provide a student-centered instructional approach, which encourages optimal skill development and increases the opportunity that individual needs will be met. This approach was recommended in 1987 in the *Alberta Secondary School Physical Education Guidelines*. Teachers anticipate that several levels of ability will be present in each class and in each sport area. By providing various progressions for skills in each activity and recognizing several levels of personal accomplishment, a higher level of participation and personal success is assured. This strategy has been implemented in the Hamilton project. With the emphasis on personal excellence, students have had the opportunity to see their own progress both within and between various proficiency levels.

Like other curriculum areas, students progress differently in all areas of physical education. By recognizing this variance, teachers plan to allow different students to assume a leadership role in assisting their peers to acquire a skill. This technique has been successfully implemented to keep more talented athletes active and personally involved in the program. Similarly, by providing a wide variety of both team and individual activities, many students in a given semester or year are afforded the opportunity to assume a leadership role.

Mosston (1981), in his book *Teaching Physical Education*, writes that many different teaching techniques should be used to ensure that each student is provided opportunities to accomplish a given task. Recognizing varied learning styles and levels of ability within each class necessitates the use of a variety of instructional approaches.

In the Hamilton program, teachers have regularly used a variety of teaching styles in physical education classes. A common technique, the command style, where all decisions are made by the teacher, is quite credible in some situations. The teacher or a selected student will demonstrate a skill, the criterion for acceptable performance is provided, and then the students are required to imitate the skill. No variation from the criterion is permitted. Students must respond on cue. This approach may appear to be rather militaristic. However, some activities such as rhythmic gymnastics, crew, and square dancing require that synchronization of the activity be established in order that the desired effect be attained.

A more flexible approach to teaching, the practice style, is similar to the command style except that the student is permitted to practice at his/her own pace. The teacher's role is to circulate and provide individual and group feedback to prevent student frustration and encourage individual success. This is the most common approach to teaching and is often used in combination with other techniques.

Another approach, the reciprocal style, is advantageous to students because it provides the opportunity to work with a peer and also receive more immediate feedback. Working in pairs, one student attempts to perform a skill while the partner makes suggestions for corrections as an observer. The observer has a criterion checklist to guide the observations and may only comment on whether or not a behavior was observed, not on the quality of the movement. Students are encouraged to make performance corrections by comparing what is observed with the checklist, and also to accept peer recommendations for improvement. The roles are then reversed, allowing each student to perform in a leadership capacity.

Another method that has been successfully employed in the Hamilton schools is the self-check approach. This approach is more individualized because it permits students to identify and correct their own errors. The teacher still explains, provides demonstrations, and gives the correct performance criteria. With the availability of video equipment, some classes are using this technology to allow students to self-check their performances. The self-check style is most commonly used in monitoring performances that occur "outside the body." For instance, throwing activities or archery can be monitored using this approach if students have a knowledge of trajectory and cause and effect relationships as they apply to a given skill. Another application is the use of mirrors to self-check. Weight rooms and dance studios have been employing this technique successfully for some time. Given the performance criterion, students can monitor their own progress using the three applications broadly mentioned.

A more student-centered technique is the inclusion style. In this style, one task (e.g., a chip shot in golf) is presented. Then each student is asked to perform the same skill, but at his/her own level of difficulty. Given the chip shot, for example, students who are just learning the skill may be asked to perform by hitting the ball from a distance of 10 feet into a target area 30 feet in diameter. After successfully completing this skill at a mastery level of perhaps 80 percent, the student would be asked to perform the same skill from an increased distance, or perhaps to aim for a smaller target. Variations other than distance and target size might be the lie of the ball or the terrain in which the ball lies. These different factors can be presented in various combinations to challenge everyone from the novice to the most experienced golfer. Similar approaches can be presented in other activity areas providing for students to feel included in an activity rather than excluded because the task was beyond their ability level. The flexibility in the achievement levels guarantees individual success and serves only to enhance personal meaning and enjoyment in the activity.

Finally, the most individualized teaching technique referred to by Mosston and implemented in the Hamilton program is the guided discovery method. In this procedure, students are challenged to discover the most effective way to perform by responding to specific questions. The questions attempt to elicit a specific skill at each student's level of ability. Festinger's (1957) Theory of Cognitive Dissonance suggests that a cognitive disturbance or perhaps a question creates the need for a solution to be found. The act of finding the solution to the question removes the dissonance. Students are asked questions to discover ideas or concepts, relationships, similarities, governing principles, systems of operation, and how's and why's.

For example, in soccer, if a teacher wanted a student to discover that by using one's toe the ball would likely go in a long and high-flying trajectory, the teacher might ask the following questions:

Q. 1. What kind of kick would be needed to pass the ball to someone who is far away?

A. 1. A long kick.

Q. 2. If there was an opposing player between the ball and the receiver, what kind of kick would be needed then?

A. 2. The ball would need to go over the opposing player.

Q. 3. Where should the ball be kicked in order to get it to go high into the air?

A. 3. Low and under the ball.

Q. 4. Which part of your foot can most comfortably get under the ball and still produce lots of force to send the ball a long way?

A. 4. The toe.

At this point, the teacher encourages the student to try this approach. This is a humanistic technique that emphasizes student mastery, accomplishment, and satisfaction (Jewett & Bain, 1985).

Using a variety of teaching techniques has been but one inviting strategy implemented in the Hamilton schools. This approach has been enthusiastically received by secondary physical education students and has been shown to increase interest and participation and decrease boredom, while developing more self-confident students.

The Role of the Teacher in Physical Education

The role of teacher is all encompassing. It is obvious that the teacher teaches. However, beyond this are decisions which weigh heavily on the success of the program and the manner in which it is perceived by the student population. There is also a philosophy of action which needs to be applied to all decisions made in physical education. Because physical fitness and wellness are critically important to personal future productivity and happiness, physical education is the natural curriculum area to address these concerns. Physical education is also the curriculum area which is charged with laying this future foundation. Unlike some academic pursuits, physical education impacts profoundly on one's life. This has been recognized in the Hamilton program. For this reason, all decisions and actions from program offering to evaluation techniques have been considered as they relate to the following question: "How does a given decision affect the students' desire to remain physically active beyond the time when they are compelled to be active?" If in response to this question, a decision is seen to be counter-productive toward this goal, then the decision would be reconsidered.

To this end, the physical education teacher must be involved in the curriculum process as an active decision-maker who responds to student needs and interests, and not blindly accept a formulated pre-packaged curriculum (Lambert, 1987). The Hamilton physical education staff did just that! They developed interesting and varied activities to create a well-balanced program. Sensitivity to current fitness trends and music and knowledge of popular activities attracted increasing numbers of students to the program, as suggested by Oberle (1988). Games were modified to increase activity levels and student success rates. For instance, instead of playing 22 players in a soccer game where the ratio of players to balls is 22:1, students often found more enjoyment in playing cross field where there were five players to the team. This dramatically addresses the need students have to be an integral part of the action. Heavy reliance on drills as the basis of activity in a gym class is typical of an elitist-type program which may develop skill level in a few, but at the expense of general student participatory decline in the program as a whole. Being part of the action far outweighs the demand for advanced skill acquisition, and this was demonstrated in an ongoing fashion by the Hamilton girls.

Students in the 1990s prefer to be active in up-to-date attire. Relaxation of stringent uniform regulations within the bounds of safety and good taste added individuality, and typically was found to be appealing to most students. The availability of good equipment was also important to students and sent the message that the school cared.

Student evaluation, when it is seen to be necessary, was also in keeping with the inclusion philosophy. Numerous types of evaluation procedures allow for individual success at the personalized levels of ability and accomplishment (Turkington & Carre, 1985). Flexibility in the school's approach to physical education evaluation has helped to generate positive feelings by communicating that people matter.

In the Hamilton program, of all the teacher qualities that students have identified as encouraging them to continue enrolling in physical education courses, the atmosphere that the teacher creates in and around the gym was seen to be most important. From the physical education office and locker rooms to the pool and the playing fields, the physical environment needs to be viewed by students as a physically and psychologically safe place and a comfort zone for everyone, not exclusively for the co-curricular "jock." Teachers promoted this feeling by portraying a relaxed and friendly attitude toward the students. Being approachable and non-judgmental encouraged students to take risks, one of which was to continue to take physical education.

The approaches to conducting physical education programs followed by the City of Hamilton schools are indeed inviting! Student needs are considered and students respond by saying through their continued attendance that physical education matters. When students no longer are obliged to be active in Hamilton, they choose to be active. What could be better evidence of an invitational program at work!

References

Alberta Department of Education. Secondary Physical Education Program of Studies. Document Resume, 1987.

Alderman, R., & Wood, N. L. An Analysis of Incentive Motivation in Young Canadian Athletes. *Canadian Journal of Applied Sports Sciences*, June, 1976, 1, 2, 169-176.

Anderson, W. G., & Barrette, G. T. What's Going On in the Gym. Motor Skills. *Theory into Practice*, 1978.

Festinger, L. *The Theory of Cognitive Dissonance*. Evanston, IL: Row, Peterson, 1957.

Fraser, L. Secondary School Physical Education: A Commitment in the 90's. Paper presented at Faculty of Education, Brock University, November, 1990.

Jewett, A. E., & Bain, L. L. *The Curriculum Process in Physical Education*. Dubuque, IA: Wm. C. Brown Publishers, College Division, 1985.

Kearns, J. The Impact of Systematic Feedback on Student Self-Esteem. Doctoral thesis, University of Alberta, Edmonton, Alberta, 1987.

Mosston, M. *Teaching Physical Education*. Toronto: Merrill Publishing Company, 1981.

Purkey, W. W., & Novak, J. M. *Inviting School Success*. Belmont, CA: Wadsworth Publishing Company, 1984.

Sawchuk, W. Keynote address at the Ontario Physical and Health Education Association Niagara Regional Meeting, MacMaster University, Hamilton, Ontario, 1989.

Turkington, H., & Carre, F. A. Individualized Physical Education. *Journal of Physical Education, Recreation and Dance*, February, 1985, 36-48.

Wilcox, R. The Failing of High School Physical Education. *Journal of Physical Education, Recreation and Dance*, Aug. 1987, 21-25.

Administrative Practices

Chapter 6
Nurturing Personally and Professionally Inviting Behaviors through a Clinical Supervision Model

By John Van Hoose and David Strahan

The invitational education theory can have an intensive impact on the improvement of instruction when it is applied to supervisory responsibilities. If instructional supervisors abide by the four propositions of trust, respect, optimism, and intentionality in their work, they will establish an atmosphere that enables teachers to be the best they can be. Supervisors can facilitate maximum teacher growth and development by applying the basic tenets of invitational education.

While encouraging teacher growth has long been a primary goal of educational supervision, meeting that goal is often difficult. Supervisors find that inviting success is very elusive for several reasons. The needs of teachers based on extent of experience varies. The tasks of teachers based on grade levels taught are very distinct. These differences are compounded due to situational variables, systemic demands, and personality differences. Three scenarios are offered to make these considerations more concrete.

Scenario One
Maggie is about to begin her first year of teaching.

She completed her teacher education in a good but typical preparation program. She had a number of courses in teaching methods, including two in language arts, one combination course in mathematics, social studies, and science practices, some background in human growth and development, philosophy, and student teaching. She is eager, excited, and very nervous. She is somewhat reserved and had difficulty controlling children during student teaching. Maggie really wants to do well with her second graders and wants to be their friend. She feels very overwhelmed with so many different preparations and is most willing to accept any suggestions from a supervisor if they will work.

Scenario Two

Susan is in her fourteenth year of teaching. She was prepared to be a secondary science teacher, but secured her initial placement at the junior high school level. She loves science, but doesn't enjoy dealing with a lot of the personal and social problems of young students. However, four years ago, the school became a middle school and the principal has emphasized the middle school concept. This means that sensitive treatment of all students has become critical. Susan has become increasingly unhappy with her work. An increasing number of parents have been complaining about the way their son/daughter has been treated by her. She is not receptive to suggestions from a supervisor.

Scenario Three

Mark is in his twenty-fourth year of teaching social studies at the senior high level. He used to be an assistant coach in football and baseball, but stopped coaching because he found it too time-consuming. He is a dynamic, knowledgeable, well-liked teacher. He frequently takes time to talk to students about their concerns. He travels a lot and has a special interest in the Civil War. He has visited every major Civil War battleground in the country. He frequently brings in materials, resources, and guest speakers to make his teaching more relevant. He is very eager to share his techniques, ideas, materials, and guidance with the other teachers at his school. His concern is that all of the other teachers seem to be so "dull" and "boring." He gets very frustrated at the lack of excitement in teaching in this school. Mark is becoming a very vocal crusader for change in instruction. Many other teachers in the school have come to view him as a major irritant and a "know-it-all." He really wants to help but feels isolated.

These three teachers reflect some of the challenges the typical supervisor may have to address in the same day. Maggie needs structure and support to develop more confidence. Susan needs to direct her energies away from "student bashing" types of behaviors, like complaining in the lounge and nagging in the classroom, toward creating a more inviting classroom. Mark needs to direct his energies away from "bashing" his colleagues toward creating a more inviting climate for growth. A supervisor may also have several dozen other teachers with a variety of needs to be addressed.

The work of the supervisor must be directed toward facilitating personal growth. However, the inordinate emphasis on attending to perceived accountability mandates through the use of carefully defined instruments which assess very specific behaviors related to teacher effectiveness may not promote the growth of the teacher. What is needed is a theoretical framework that lays the foundation for a supervisory approach that promotes effective teaching and personal growth. This chapter will provide the needed foundation and the framework to promote growth and effective teaching in Maggie, Susan, Mark, and most other teachers with a multitude of diverse needs.

Theoretical Framework

One of the advantages of invitational education as a framework for supervision is its potential for encouraging both teacher effectiveness and personal growth. First articulated by Purkey (1978), invitational education integrates self-concept theories with research on teaching. The result is a framework for analyzing teaching that emphasizes both effective teaching practices and personal growth and development. This emphasis on "the person in the process" (Purkey & Novak, 1984, p. 72) makes invitational education especially conducive to both clinical supervision and self-assessment.

The basic premise of invitational education is that teachers can encourage students to view themselves more positively and learn more efficiently by "inviting" success. Through the messages they send, teachers can foster positive perceptions and encourage active learning. Invitational teaching stems from positive perceptions of students and a consistent behavioral "stance." Purkey and Novak (1984) suggest that these inviting perceptions and stance provide the basis for a wide range of "personally" and "professionally" inviting practices" (p. 72).

As Purkey (1991) points out, invitational education is based on the four propositions of trust, respect, optimism, and intentionality (Purkey, p. 1). He goes on to point out that there must be recognition of the interdependence of people and that everyone in a school setting must function in a cooperative, collaborative manner. He asserts that we must believe and act on the notion that all people are able, valuable, and responsible. This is extended to include the perspective that all people have untapped potential in all areas. He ends by emphasizing that we must carefully study the places, policies, processes and programs, and people to ensure that the tenets of invitational education are being fully implemented. In this way, educators will become both personally and professionally inviting. Amos (1985) elaborates the distinction between these two dimensions, defining personally inviting practices as those which "encourage students to feel good about themselves and their abilities in general" and professionally inviting practices as those which "encourage students to learn and appreciate course content" (p. 2).

In order to assess such practices, Amos, Purkey, and Tobias (1984) developed the *Invitational Teaching Survey*. They began by identifying potentially inviting practices from the literature and soliciting the ratings of 219 experts in invitational education. Factor analysis of the resulting 43 items yielded five subscores: consideration, commitment, coordination, proficiency, and expectation. Using this instrument, Amos (1985) surveyed 1045 dental hygiene students and found positive relationships between inviting teacher practices and student affective outcome measures. The teachers who were rated higher on both personal and professional dimensions demonstrated higher student outcomes.

A range of investigations have explored the linkages between inviting practices and teacher effectiveness. Associations with affective outcomes have been especially well-documented in postsecondary settings (Inglis, 1976; Ripley, 1985; Smith, 1985). Lambeth (1980) and Turner (1983) found significant correlations between perceived teacher behaviors and student achievement in secondary school settings. Each of these studies has used student ratings of teacher performance as the basis for defining inviting practices.

Identifying Inviting Practices

The success of the *Invitational Teaching Survey* in postsecondary settings led us to begin a search for specific inviting practices that might provide a framework for supervision of elementary, middle, and secondary teachers. We identified five major reviews of the literature on teacher effectiveness that, while not reported in terms of "invitations," suggested that personally and professionally inviting practices contribute substantially to student achievement in elementary and secondary education (Barnes, 1981; Brophy, 1983; Fisher, 1978; Johnston, 1984; Rosenshine, 1983). Fisher and others (1978) conducted a seven-year investigation of teaching in which they described specific ways that teachers promote "academic learning time," maintaining student involvement with tasks they can complete with high rates of success.

The authors described effective practices within such major functions as diagnosis, prescription, presentation, activity, and monitoring. An essential characteristic of the effective teachers in this series of investigations was their ability to establish an "academic context" for their classrooms, a shared expectation that learning would occur. Barnes (1981) identified twelve investigations of specific teaching practices that related to measured outcomes in student achievement. From these studies, Barnes identified 83 teaching practices documented in two or more investigations. Brophy (1983) reviewed 66 studies of effective teaching practices. Rosenshine (1983) reviewed 48 similar studies and identified six major clusters of "instructional functions." Johnston (1984) reviewed many of these same studies and added conclusions based on direct observations of exemplary schools.

These studies suggest that successful teachers invite students to view themselves more positively and to learn more efficiently through an interaction of professional skills in planning instruction, presenting lessons, organizing activities, monitoring performance, and providing feedback. These teachers also invite student success through clusters of personally inviting skills that foster positive contexts for learning. Through the interaction of these skills, successful teachers create classroom environments that are exciting, inviting places to learn.

We found a strong correspondence between practices identified as "effective" in these studies and practices identified as "inviting" in the *Invitational Teaching Survey*. Using survey items as a starting point, we drafted the *Invitational Teaching Observation Instrument* (ITOI) (Strahan & Van Hoose, 1987). We conducted two pilot studies to test the validity and reliability of this instrument (Strahan & Van Hoose, 1986; 1987). To assess the concurrent validity of the items on the ITOI, we cross-referenced our items with items from two performance appraisal systems and with practices identified in the five major studies of teacher effectiveness that we reviewed. One of the appraisal systems, the *Assessments of Performance in Teaching Observation Instrument* (Stulak et al., 1982) was developed by the South Carolina Educator Improvement Task Force and was derived from a review of more than 50 state and national teacher evaluation forms. This instrument provided a prototype format (each item accompanied by a set of descriptors and space to record examples of the behaviors).

This "binary" system was selected in preference to a numerical rating scale to reinforce the emphasis on self-assessment and clinical supervision rather than evaluation of teaching. The other appraisal system, the *Teacher Performance Appraisal System* (Stuck et al., 1984) was adopted by the state of North Carolina as the basis for the evaluation of teaching. It, too, was based on a review of other teacher appraisal systems and based on an extensive review of the literature. These two appraisal systems provided a basis for analyzing the items selected from the *Invitational Teaching Survey* and from the review of the literature. All items were cross-referenced with these appraisal systems and exceptions noted. Results are reported in the appendix to this chapter.

Videotapes generated in the pilot study provided the basis for reliability assessment. Instructional supervisors and teachers in graduate-level supervision and instruction programs served as raters for two subsequent analyses of reliability with a different videotaped lesson. The first group consisted of 11 instructional supervisors selected for their experience in education (average of 6.9 years of supervision). Each member of this group had also been trained in the use of at least one other performance appraisal system. The second group consisted of 10 experienced teachers with an average of 9.8 years of experience in classrooms K-12. The protocols for each behavior on the instrument were categorized as "demonstrated," "not demonstrated," or "no opportunity to observe." Percentages of agreement were then computed and items with composite percentages of agreement of less than 70 were dropped from the instrument. Supervisors and teachers also responded to a survey regarding the use of the instrument. Details regarding the assessment of validity and reliability are reported in the appendix to this chapter.

The results of our pilot studies demonstrate that the ITOI is a valid representation of the research on teacher effectiveness and provides a useful framework for analyzing instruction. The ITOI demonstrates strong construct and concurrent validity. The reviews of research cited in the development of the instrument suggest that the 32 practices identified in the revised instrument are associated with student achievement at elementary, middle, and secondary levels. All 32 behaviors are supported by at least two of the five reviews. While their purposes are different, the teacher performance appraisal systems reviewed provide support for all but four of the 32 practices. This convergence of information suggests that this instrument is a useful starting point for extending successful teaching. Figure 1 on pages 106 and 107 provides a listing of the practices identified.

From these studies, we concluded that the ITOI is a potentially useful instrument for observing and analyzing teachers' inviting practices for both clinical and collegial supervision. These practices may promote both academic and affective growth. As suggested by raters, the instrument may be most useful with peer supervision. It may be especially useful with voluntary assessment rather than as a tool for mandatory evaluation.

We have used the *Model For Inviting Success in the Classroom* with preservice and inservice teachers as a basis for analyzing instruction. As we concluded in a report of our efforts in the *Middle School Journal* (Strahan & Van Hoose, 1988):

> The picture of successful teaching that emerges from these investigations is that of a caring and dynamic professional who understands students, plans lessons accordingly, presents lessons in a systematic fashion, involves all students in a range of learning activities, monitors their performance carefully, and provides feedback in a supportive fashion. (p. 3)

This model can be applied to the real world of Maggie, Susan and Mark. Maggie needs to be in a setting that instills confidence and encourages experimentation. If she experiences tangible support from a supervisor, she is more likely to maintain her poise and be patient with her students. She will be more inclined to share more of who she is with her children. In short, she will demonstrate the personally inviting behaviors outlined. This, in turn, will enable her to develop professionally inviting behaviors, especially in the areas of planning and presentation. Incorporating these practices into her lessons and encouraging more active involvement will assist her in class management.

Susan, in contrast, may need to focus much more extensively on developing enthusiasm for learning. She already enjoys her subject, but has not linked teaching with learning. The notion of modelling courtesy and respect for students has not occurred to

Figure 1
A Model for Inviting Success in the Classroom

Professionally Inviting Practices

Planning
The teacher is prepared for class.
· accommodates individual differences in learning rates.
· accommodates individual differences in learning styles.
· plans varied activities for a single lesson.
· plans a systematic progression for the lesson.
· plans clear transitions between activities.

Presentation
The teacher presents the lesson in an inviting fashion.
· begins the lesson promptly.
· provides an overview.
· uses motivating techniques to generate interest.
· structures the lesson in logical steps.
· speaks in a manner that facilitates student learning.
· uses personalized references for illustrations.
· makes smooth transitions between activities.
· communicates purpose and meaning of the lesson.
· uses a variety of instructional activities during a single lesson.

Active Involvement
The teacher promotes active involvement by all students.
· encourages students to express personal ideas and interests.
· provides all students opportunity to practice new skills.
· asks varied and appropriate questions.
· waits for students to respond to questions.
· asks reflective questions that stimulate thinking.

Feedback
The teacher provides students feedback on their progress and performance.
· praises student performance and expresses appreciation to students.
· demonstrates support when responding to student errors.

Monitoring
The teacher adjusts presentations and activities in response to feedback from students.
· responds to students with special problems.
· monitors student performance to determine needs for clarification, assistance, or adjustment.
· addresses disruptions that interfere with student learning.

Figure 1 (continued)
A Model for Inviting Success in the Classroom

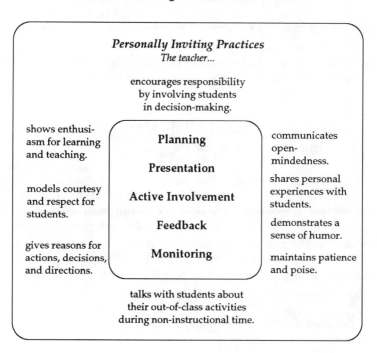

her. She was not taught that way. Over the years, she has developed planning and presentation skills, but has not reflected deeply on the personally inviting practices that can help create a classroom climate that encourages "academic learning time." If she can create a context where she feels students are more involved in learning, she will be more inclined to see students' strengths and less likely to engage in "student bashing" verbal behaviors.

Mark understands the importance of personally and professionally inviting behaviors with students. However, his vehemence about changing the instruction of all teachers has caused him to be insensitive to the needs of other teachers. If he can begin to reflect more deeply on the larger "context" for teaching, he may be able to direct more of his energy toward team-building and less toward "colleague bashing."

Invitational education includes a series of beliefs that apply to life with adults as well as students. The principles can't be limited to interactions with our clientele. They must direct our life with colleagues as well.

Clinical and Invitational Supervision: Inviting Teachers to Grow

It is our contention that this perspective and many of these behaviors are not only appropriate but essential for the supervisor who wishes to maximize the effectiveness of each teacher. As Glickman states, "the supervisors must work with the teachers in the same developmental manner that teachers are expected to work with their students" (Glickman, 1981, p. 62). If the supervisor wants to be attuned to what is best for the teacher, then the following behaviors will be **most appropriate.**

Personally and Professionally Inviting Supervisory Behavior

Trust
The Supervisor:
◆ asks reflective questions that stimulate thinking;
◆ allows for wait time for the teacher to reflect before commenting;
◆ uses personalized references for illustration;
◆ expresses praise and appreciation for desirable teaching behaviors;

◆ provides ample opportunities for active involvement by the teacher;
◆ communicates open-mindedness.

Intentionality

The Supervisor:
◆ is prepared for the preconference, the class observation and postconference;
◆ arrives on time and is ready to begin promptly;
◆ provides an overview of the intent of the process;
◆ provides a logical overview of the process;
◆ uses motivating techniques to sustain interest;
◆ summarizes the process and highlights the target areas for improvement.

Respect

The Supervisor:
◆ speaks in a manner that facilitates learning;
◆ listens and attends carefully to the concerns of the teacher;
◆ adjusts input based on the teacher's reflections and reactions;
◆ allows for differences in teacher learning styles and rates;
◆ demonstrates support when responding to teacher concerns;
◆ shares personal experiences with teacher;
◆ talks with teacher about out-of-class interests and concerns both personal and professional;
◆ models courtesy and respect for the teacher;
◆ maintains patience and poise;
◆ gives reasons for all recommendations;
◆ encourages responsibility by involving teachers

in decision-making;

◆ gives reasons for all recommendations.

Optimism

The Supervisor:

◆ focuses on the positive and suggests areas for improvement;

◆ encourages teachers to express personal ideas, needs, and
interests;

◆ shows enthusiasm for teaching and learning;

◆ demonstrates a sense of humor.

These behaviors bring the basic tenets of invitational education to life in the supervisory process. They reflect the trust, intentionality, respect, and optimism that are the cornerstones of this perspective. To ensure that these behaviors occur, a supervisory system that is anchored in the needs of teachers must be implemented. Clinical supervision attends to the concerns just outlined.

A Review of Clinical Supervision

A perspective must be found that will maximize the interactions between supervisors and teachers. One model that holds great promise for maximum interaction is the *Clinical Supervision Model*. "The purposes—and therefore the expected benefits—of Clinical Supervision are improvement of instruction and development of the teacher" (Sullivan, 1980, p. 11). It is important to note the emphasis in the individual **growth** of the teacher as well as instructional improvement. The stages in the model, according to Cogan (1973), are presented in Figure 2.

In these stages, there are substantial opportunities for the supervisor to carefully analyze the unique strengths and needs of the teacher, and there are ample opportunities to interact with the

Figure 2
The Traditional Clinical Supervision Process

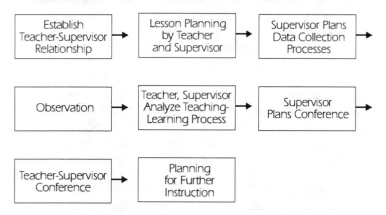

teacher. The interactions provide the forum in which extensive modeling of inviting behaviors can occur and lead to instructional improvement and teacher development.

Given the potential for substantial positive results, it seems reasonable to assume that the model, which is rather well-known, is being utilized. However, that is not the case. There are several barriers which must be negotiated before utilizing any form of clinical supervision. The most serious of these obstacles are that: 1) supervision is a most time-consuming endeavor, 2) there is not a sufficient number of staff members to deal adequately with all teachers, and 3) the administrators in most schools have been given more and more administrative service responsibilities and have less and less time for instructional supervision. The result is that a lot of monitoring takes place, but substantial instructional improvement is less likely to occur (Glatthorn, 1984). This is due to the fact that monitoring deals more with preventing or eliminating the negative and less with nurturing the positive. As a result, instructional feedback patterns on how to make a topic more inviting and exciting to young adolescents are not provided on an ongoing basis. Due to systemic restraints, clinical supervision and other models that may lead to extensive long-lasting instructional improvement and teacher growth are not commonly used. If the clinical model could be modified to address these major barriers, the contribution to the education profession could be substantial.

One approach that is clinical in nature and provides some reduction in the costs in time, money, and personnel is peer clinical supervision. A recent study conducted in a private school involved the implementation of all eight steps of the model with successful results (McFaul & Cooper, 1984). This experiment conveys that clinical supervision can be modified to extend the role of the supervisor to teachers. Since middle level supervisors cannot work with all teachers on a one-to-one continuous basis, a way to expand the number of "supervisors" must be provided. The *Teacher Improvement Process* (Van Hoose & Strahan, 1986) accomplishes this goal through a streamlined version of the process. This model addresses systemic restraints which promote instructional supervision and maximizes teacher development.

The Teacher Improvement Process

Though the Teacher Improvement Process (TIP) can be taught at many levels, its application must be at the school level. The school is the primary unit of change (Goodlad, 1975). It is at this level that the needs and problems of young adolescents can be isolated, addressed, and attended to in a manageable way. Implementing an instructional plan at a higher level can lead to identifying concerns that are too global to address or can lead to attending to needs that are present in one school setting, but not in other schools.

To implement this plan, we are calling for resurrecting the role of the principal-teacher (or, if more appropriate, the assistant principal-teacher), making this person the primary resource for teachers in a school. Many middle school principals may be concerned that they are not experts in all content areas—i.e., language arts, mathematics, physical education—but that need not be a concern. They do not have to be content experts; they have to be human relations experts and they have to be or become process experts. A description of the TIP, including how middle level principals and supervisors are to be involved, follows.

TIP is a broad plan of action involving several teachers working together to help each other improve in their instructional efforts. The ideal range of teachers is from three to six. The team includes a leader, who should be a principal or other supervisor, who is sensitive to both the personal and professional needs of the participants. All members agree to: 1) participate as fully as possible in the process, 2) be observed by the others in the group, 3) provide constructive feedback to other members, and 4) attend to feedback about their own teaching from others in the group. The TIP process includes four stages, as depicted in Figure 3.

Figure 3
Stages in the Teacher Improvement Process

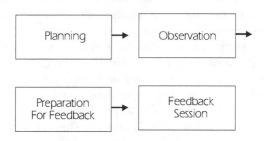

Following is a brief description of each stage in the TIP:

Stage 1 - Planning
 ◆ A teacher agrees to be the observed teacher for this session.
 ◆ He/she describes a problem area and an objective (e.g., whenever I ask questions, no one answers them, or in social studies advisor/advisee, no one wants to offer their opinions).
 ◆ A plan of instruction is provided by the teacher to be observed.
 ◆ The team analyzes the plan of action, clarifies concerns, and decides various data collection methods to be used.
 ◆ The teacher indicates whether his/her concerns will be attended to through the use of the methods outlined and discusses any additional concerns to be considered.

Stage 2 - The Observation
 ◆ The purpose of this stage is to gather objective information (data) that will help the teacher being observed. If possible, the class should be video-taped and one of the team members needs to know how to run the VCR equipment. That is, one person should plan to be present while the teacher is performing. If video tape equipment is not available, the teachers could visit the critiqued teacher on different days or at different times during the same day, depending on whether the teacher's concern is with a specific class or with a topic covered in several classes. The live visits should not take place simultaneously because it is too disruptive. If different classes are to be visited,

additional lesson plans need to be provided. The guideline is for the teacher to indicate those classes or times when his/her immediate concern exists. The observations should then be structured around this. In a team setting, which is fairly common in middle schools, scheduling concerns are usually minimal.

Stage 3 - Preparation

◆ The teacher does a critique of the class(es) on his/her own. This includes viewing the videotape in private. Strengths and weaknesses are written out.

◆ Other members of the team meet and reflect together on the performance.

◆ If videotaped, each person views the videotape at his/her convenience prior to meeting with the group.

◆ It is often very interesting to compare a principal's analysis to the teacher's analyses. Objective data and subjective information are reported and analysis is made. Strengths as well as shortcomings are carefully and sensitively considered. The personal state of readiness of the performing teacher is considered in determining how many problem areas to cover. No one should be taken farther than they can go. No one should be bludgeoned with data about weaknesses that they are not ready to consider. Careful attention is given to relating the plan of action to the overall objective(s). All criticisms to be made should be backed up by data.

Stage 4 - Feedback Session

◆ The teacher always reports his/her findings first. If there are discrepancies between the teacher's perceptions and the team analysis, the principal or supervisor (the team leader) reassesses the analysis and, given the state of readiness of the teacher, asks for the segments of the reports most useful at this time. If the teacher becomes defensive during the critique session, the team leader takes the appropriate action to allay anxiety on the part of the teacher.

◆ An analysis of the entire TIP is made at the conclusion of this session and another teacher decides to be the next teacher to be observed.

If TIP is implemented properly, the needs of diverse teachers can be addressed. This is so because the process begins with the unique needs of the participants. It is possible for Maggie to belong to a TIP group that gives her the support and guidance which enables her to gain the self-confidence to be both personally and professionally inviting. It is also possible for Mark to become more sensitive to his colleagues and be a powerful catalyst for positive growth in fellow teachers. It even becomes possible for Susan to begin to consider the critical importance of addressing the unique personal and social needs of middle school students. If she is a part of a group of teachers who are attuned to the overall needs of students, she may absorb some of this type of mentality through osmosis due to regular contact with these teachers.

This process has been and is being used in schools and it works. It can be directed toward general instructional strategies that bridge all subject areas or it can be geared toward unique concerns in one subject area or it can focus on one particular class of students. Each teacher can be observed at least three times a year and all teachers in each group are continually involved in instructional improvement activities. A combination of these interactions, as depicted in Figure 4, could be a focal point for observation. An observation instrument could be used like the type used in a number of states to evaluate teaching performance. This can help a teacher, especially a beginning teacher, feel more prepared and less anxious about the required evaluation activities by the official evaluator(s). However, the intent of this effort is to provide a formative, not a summative evaluation. Other instruments, such as the *Barbour Scale* which includes procedural, subject-related, and affective categories, could also be used. Or, it may be determined that field notes or anecdotal comments would be more appropriate.

Figure 4
Interactions in the Teacher Improvement Process

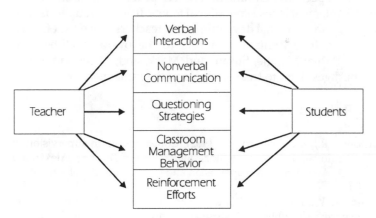

Conclusion

Lounsbury and Vars state that "teaching is so basic a profession that everyone knows what it is; yet it is so infinitely complex and multidimensional that it is nearly impossible to define adequately" (Lounsbury & Vars, 1978, p. 2). Perhaps we tend to attend to the basic and simpler dimensions that we know and can categorize and refrain from dealing with the subtleties and complexities of the art of teaching. Perhaps we need to grapple with issues such as genuineness and authenticity in teaching and supervision. The time is right for us to explore how to help teachers become more professionally and personally inviting in the classroom (Purkey, 1984) with their students. The model for inviting success presented in this chapter is a realistic mechanism to use to guide supervisory efforts. The only way to reach a large number of teachers with this type of message through a process that is built on Trust, Intentionality, Respect, and Optimism. The TIP process is a flexible model that implements these invitational tenets. It enables supervisors to promote the personal development of teachers as well as effective teaching. It legitimizes attending to the overall well-being of teachers like Maggie, Susan, and Mark, and, at the same time, encourages them to treat students in the same manner.

References

Alfonso, R., & Goldsberry, L. (1982). Colleagueship in supervision. In Sergiovanni, Thomas (editor), *Supervision of Teaching*. Alexandria, VA: Association for Supervision and Curriculum Development, 90-107.

Amos, L. W., Purkey, W. W., & Tobias, N. (1984). Invitational teaching survey. Unpublished instrument. University of North Carolina at Greensboro.

Amos, L. (1985). Professionally and personally inviting teacher practices as related to affective course outcomes. Doctoral dissertation. University of North Carolina at Greensboro.

Bailey, G. (1981). *Teacher self-assessment: A means for improving classroom instruction.* Washington, DC: National Education Association. ERIC number ED 207 967.

Barnes, S. (1981). *Synthesis of selected research on teaching findings.* Austin, TX: Research and Development Center for Teacher Education.

Brophy, J. (1983). Classroom organization and management. *Elementary School Journal,* 83(4).

Cogan, M. L. (1973). *Clinical Supervision.* Boston, MA: Houghton Mifflin Company.

Eisner, E. W. (1982). An artistic approach to supervision. In Sergiovanni, Thomas (editor), *Supervision of Teaching.* Alexandria, VA: Association for Supervision and Curriculum Development, 53-66.

Fisher, C. W., *et al.* (1978). *Teaching and learning in the elementary school: A summary of the beginning teacher evaluation study.* Study Report VII-1. San Francisco, CA: Far West Laboratory for Educational Research and Development.

Garman, N. (1982). The clinical approach to supervision. In Sergiovanni, Thomas (editor), *Supervision of Teaching.* Alexandria, VA: Association for Supervision and Curriculum Development, 35-53.

Glatthorn, A. A. (1984). *Differentiated supervision.* Alexandria, VA: Association for Supervision and Curriculum Development.

Glickman, C. D. (1981). *Developmental supervision.* Alexandria, VA: Association for Supervision and Curriculum Development.

Goodlad, J. (1975). *Dynamics of educational change.* New York: McGraw Hill.

Inglis, S. C. (1976). The development and validation of an instrument to assess teacher invitations and teacher effectiveness as reported by students in a technical and general post-secondary educational setting. Unpublished doctoral dissertation, University of Florida, Gainesville.

Johnston, H. J. (1984). A synthesis of research findings on middle level education. In Lounsbury, J. (editor), *Perspectives in Middle School Education, 1964-1984.* Columbus, OH: National Middle School Association, 134-157.

Krenapfel, B. (1984, September). Supervision of curriculum at the middle level. *NASSP Bulletin,* 68(473), 52-57.

Lambeth, C. R. (1980). Teacher invitations and effectiveness as reported by secondary students in Virginia. Unpublished doctoral dissertation, University of Virginia at Charlottesville.

Lounsbury, J. H., & Vars, G. E. (1978). *A curriculum for the middle school years*. New York: Harper and Row.

Marks, J. R., Stoops, E., & King-Stoops, J. (1971). *Handbook of educational supervision: A guide for the practitioner*. Boston, MA: Allyn and Bacon.

McFaul, S. A., & Cooper, J. M. (1984, April). Peer clinical supervision: Theory and reality. *Educational Leadership*, 41(7), 4-9.

McNergney, R. F., & Carrier, C. A. (1981). *Teacher development*. New York: Macmillan.

Merenbloom, E. Y. (1984, September). Staff development: The key to effective middle level schools. *NASSP Bulletin*, 68(473), 25-33.

Purkey, W. W. (1978). *Inviting school success: A self-concept approach to teaching and learning*. Belmont, CA: Wadsworth.

Purkey, W. W., & Novak, J. M. (1984). *Inviting school success*. Belmont, CA: Wadsworth.

Purkey, W. W. (1991). *What is Invitational Education and how does it work?* Greensboro, NC: University of North Carolina Greensboro.

Reavis, C. A. (1978). Research in review/clinical supervision, *Educational Leadership*, 35, 580-584.

Ripley, D. M. (1985). Invitational teaching behaviors in the associate degree clinical setting. Unpublished master's thesis, University of North Carolina at Greensboro.

Rosenshine, B. (1983). Teaching functions in instructional programs. *The Elementary School Journal*, 83(4).

Sergiovanni, T. J. (1982). Toward a theory of supervisory practice: Integrating scientific, clinical, and artistic views. In Sergiovanni, Thomas (editor), *Supervision of Teaching*. Alexandria, VA: Association for Supervision and Curriculum Development, 67-77.

Smith, C. (1985). The effect of selected teaching practices on affective outcomes of graduate nursing students: An extension and replication. Unpublished master's thesis, University of North Carolina at Greensboro.

Squire, J. R. (1964). The response of adolescents while reading four short stories. Urbana, IL: National Council of Teachers of English.

Strahan, D., & Van Hoose, J. (1986). The development of clinical supervision procedures for extending the personally and professionally inviting behaviors of middle grades teachers—a pilot study. Paper presented at American Educational Research Association, San Francisco, CA.

Strahan, D., & Van Hoose, J. (1987). The development of an instrument to assess teaching practices that invite success. Paper presented at American Educational Research Association, Washington, DC.

Strahan, D., & Van Hoose, J. (1988). Inviting student and teacher renewal. *Middle School Journal*, 19 (3), 3-6.

Stuck, G., and others. (1985). *Teacher performance appraisal system*. Raleigh, NC: State Department of Public Instruction.

Stulac, J. F., *et al.* (1982). Assessments of performance in teaching observation instrument. Columbia, SC: South Carolina Educator Improvement Task Force.

Sullivan, C. G. (1980). *Clinical supervision: A state of the art review*. Alexandria, VA: Association for Supervision and Curriculum Development.

Turner, R. B. (1983). Teacher invitations and effectiveness as reported by physical education students. Unpublished doctoral dissertation, University of North Carolina at Greensboro.

Appendix

Validation of the Invitational Teaching Observation Instrument

Analyses and revision of original items for construct validity produced a list of 35 inviting practices. Table 1 on pages 122 and 123 presents an overview of these behaviors as they relate to the five selected reviews of research. Evidence for the effectiveness of each of these behaviors is provided in at least two of the reviews of the literature analyzed.

Analysis of these items for concurrent validity is also summarized in Table 1. Thirty of the 35 inviting practices were included in at least one of the teacher appraisal systems analyzed. Two of the exceptions ("waits for responses" and "asks reflective questions") were retained because they were so strongly referenced in the literature. The other 3 exceptions ("shares personal experiences,"

TABLE 1
Selected variables from research on teaching
related to inviting practices

Systems	Reviews of Research					Teacher Appraisal			
	Amos	Barnes	Brophy	Fisher	Johnston	Purkey	Rosenshine	TPAS	APT
Planning									
1. Is prepared for class (1)	✓			✓				✓	✓
2. Accommodates differences in rate (16)	✓			✓	✓				✓
3. Accommodates differences in style (17)	✓				✓				✓
Presentation									
4. Begins the lesson promptly (2)	✓	✓	✓					✓	✓
5. Provides an overview (3)	✓	✓			✓			✓	✓
6. Uses motivating techniques (13)		✓			✓			✓	✓
7. Speaks in a facilitating manner (4)	✓			✓				✓	✓
8. Structures lesson logically (5)	✓	✓		✓			✓		✓
9. Makes smooth transitions (6)	✓	✓	✓					✓	
10. Uses personalized references (8)	✓				✓			✓	✓
11. Uses a variety of activities (9)	✓				✓				✓
12. Summarizes major points (26)	✓				✓			✓	
Active Involvement									
13. Provides active involvement (14)		✓				✓	✓		✓
14. Provides skills practice (15)		✓					✓		✓
15. Asks varied and appropriate questions (10)		✓		✓	✓		✓	✓	✓
16. Asks reflective questions (12)	✓	✓			✓	✓			
[17.] Waits for responses (11)									
17. Encourages personal expression (24)		✓			✓				✓
18. Encourages responsibility (32)	✓		✓		✓				

TABLE 1 (continued)

Systems	Reviews of Research					Teacher Appraisal			
	Amos	Barnes	Brophy	Fisher	Johnston	Purkey	Rosenshine	TPAS	APT
Monitoring									
19. Monitors student performance (20)		✓		✓	✓			✓	✓
20. Addresses disruptions (21)		✓			✓			✓	✓
21. Responds to special problems (22)	✓			✓	✓		✓		
22. Adjusts presentations (7)					✓		✓	✓	✓
Feedback									
23. Provides feedback on progress (19)		✓		✓	✓		✓	✓	✓
24. Praises student performance (20)	✓	✓			✓				
25. Demonstrates support - errors (23)					✓		✓		
26. Gives reasons for actions (34)	✓	✓							✓
Personal Factors									
27. Shows enthusiasm for learning (30)	✓				✓				✓
28. Communicates purpose and meaning (25)	✓	✓			✓			✓	✓
29. Shares personal experiences (27)	✓				✓				
30. Models courtesy and respect (31)	✓				✓				✓
31. Maintains patience and poise (33)	✓				✓				✓
32. Talks about out-of-class activities (28)	✓				✓				
[33.] Demonstrates a sense of humor (29)	✓				✓				✓
[34.] Communicates open-mindedness (35)	✓	✓			✓				✓

( ) Parentheses indicate numbers on original instrument.
[ ] Brackets indicate items eliminated.

"talks with students about out-of-class activities," and "encourages responsibility") were retained because earlier studies suggest that they contribute significantly to students' perceptions of self-esteem (Amos, 1985; Ripley, 1985; Smith, 1985). These five items were marked with a scope note since they did not demonstrate the same degree of concurrent validity as the other 30 items.

Reliability

Table 2, on pages 125, 126, and 127, presents the results of reliability analysis. As indicated in Table 2, the average percentage of agreement among the supervisors' group was 88.88. The average percentage of agreement among teachers was 89.43. Composite percentages of agreement for each item on all three analyses of reliability ranged from 66.3 to 100. Three items with composite percentages of agreement of less than 70 percent were dropped from the instrument. The resulting 32-item instrument yields a composite percentage of agreement of 91.08.

Teachers and supervisors were also asked to indicate whether or not they considered the instrument useful by colleagues in peer supervision, by instructional supervisors, and by evaluators in mandatory evaluation. All of the respondents rated the *Invitational Teaching Observation Instrument* useful in peer supervision; 96 percent rated it useful in evaluations by supervisors to improve instruction; 50 percent rated it useful in mandatory evaluations.

Invitational Teaching Observation Instrument

The *Invitational Teaching Observation Instrument* represents a synthesis of research on effective teaching and the concept of invitational education (Purkey & Novak, 1984). The instrument consists of 32 descriptors of teacher behaviors and guidelines for observing them. These descriptors are based on seven major reviews of investigations of teacher effectiveness. Each of these

TABLE 2
Ratings of Supervisors and Teachers in Second Lesson
and Percentages of Agreement

	Demon-strated		Not Demon-strated		No oppor-tunity to observe		Percentage Agreement			Com-posite
	spr	tch	spr	tch	spr	tch	spr	tch	orig	
Planning										
1. Is prepared for class (1)	11	10	0	0	0	0	100	100	88	96.0
2. Accomodates differences in rate (16)	10	7	0	1	1	2	91	70	59	73.3
3. Accommodates differences in style (17)	9	8	0	2	2	0	73	80	65	72.7
Presentation										
4. Begins the lesson promptly (2)	10	9	0	0	1	1	91	90	59	80.0
5. Provides an overview (3)	11	10	0	0	0	0	100	100	82	94.0
6. Uses motivating techniques (13)	11	10	0	0	0	0	100	100	53	84.3
7. Speaks in a facilitating manner (4)	11	10	0	0	0	0	100	100	94	98.0
8. Structures lesson logically (5)	11	10	0	0	0	0	100	100	76	92.0
9. Makes smooth transitions (6)	11	10	0	0	0	0	100	100	82	94.0
10. Uses personalized references (8)	11	9	0	1	0	0	100	90	65	85.0
11. Uses a variety of activities (9)	11	10	0	0	0	0	100	100	100	100
12. Summarizes major points (26)	2	3	2	0	7	7	64	70	88	74.0

TABLE 2 (Continued)

Active Involvement

13. Provides active involvement (14)	11	10	0	0	0	0	100	100	65	88.3
14. Provides skills practice (15)	11	10	0	0	0	0	100	100	53	84.3
15. Asks varied and appropriate questions (10)	10	5	1	4	0	1	91		76	72.3
16. Asks reflective questions (12)	10	8	1	2	0	0	91	80	59	76.7
[17.] Waits for responses (11)	7	6	2	2	2	2	64	60	76	66.7
17. Encourages personal expression (24)	11	10	0	0	0	0	100	100	76	92.0
18. Encourages responsibility (32)	10	8	0	0	1	2	91	80	82	84.3

Monitoring

19. Monitors student performance (20)	11	10	0	0	0	0	100	100	88	96.0
20. Addresses disruptions (21)	2	1	0	1	9	8	82	80	100	87.3
21. Responds to special problems (22)	2	8	1	0	8	2	73	80	88	80.3
22. Adjusts presentations (7)	10	2	0	0	1	8	91	80	59	76.7

TABLE 2 (Continued)

Feedback

23. Provides feedback on progress (19)	11	10	0	0	0	0	100	100	88	96.0
24. Praises student performance (20)	11	10	0	0	0	0	100	100	82	94.0
25. Demonstrates support - errors (23)	8	3	1	0	1	7	73	70	82	75.0
26. Gives reasons for actions (34)	6	10	3	0	2	0	54	100	76	76.7

Personal Factors

27. Shows enthusiasm for learning (30)	11	9	0	0	0	1	100	90	59	83.0
28. Communicates purpose and meaning (25)	10	10	0	0	1	0	91	100	88	93.0
29. Shares personal experiences (27)	11	10	0	0	0	0	100	100	59	86.3
30. Models courtesy and respect (31)	11	10	0	0	0	0	100	100	82	94.0
31. Maintains patience and poise (33)	10	10	0	0	1	0	91	100	88	93.0
32. Talks about out-of-class activities (28)	2	1	0	0	9	9	82	90	94	88.7
[33.] Demonstrates a sense of humor (29)	1	0	4	2	6	8	54	80	65	66.3
[34.] Communicates open-mindedness (35)	7	9	1	0	3	1	64	90	53	69.0

( ) Parentheses indicate numbers on original instrument.
[ ] Brackets indicate items eliminated.

descriptors has been associated with student performance in at least two of these major reviews. Thirty of these descriptors have been further validated through cross-referencing with two comprehensive performance appraisal instruments (*Assessments Performance in Teaching*, 1982; *Teacher Performance Appraisal System*, 1985). The four exceptions are noted (*) and are included in this instrument because they have such strong support in the literature. The descriptors are organized by performance categories (planning, presentation, active involvement, monitoring, feedback, and personal factors) to provide a framework for analyzing specific ways in which teachers encourage student success. The extensive research basis for these descriptors strongly suggests that teachers who demonstrate many of these behaviors will be effective in providing a successful climate for learning.

Planning

1. The teacher is prepared for class. (1, 4, 8, 9)
The teacher has developed strategies for achieving each objective. These strategies are reflected in written plans. Such strategies may include activities, games, demonstrations, discussions, lectures. The teacher provides sufficient information for the observer to determine if strategies address objectives. The focus is on the intent of the objective. Even if objectives are not written, procedures should be appropriate for the intent of the objective.

2. Accommodates individual differences in learning rates (1, 4, 5, 9)
In both plans and procedures, the teacher provides for differences among students in rates of completing tasks. Activities are provided for students who finish work early and opportunities are available for students who need time later in the lesson to complete assignments.

3. Accommodates individual differences in learning styles (1, 5, 9)

In both plans and procedures, the teacher provides for differences among students in preferred modalities and methods of organizing information. For example, every lesson should incorporate some opportunity for visual, auditory, and kinesthetic/tactile experiences. Lessons should also provide some concrete activities as well as discussion of more abstract ideas.

Presentation

4. Begins the lesson promptly (1, 2, 3, 8, 9)
The time for beginning the lesson is indicated on the schedule. A minimum of instructional time should be used for clerical tasks such as checking attendance. The behavior is not demonstrated if instructional time is used for such things as organizing needed materials.

5. Provides an overview (1, 2, 5, 7, 8, 9)
The instructional plan includes an orientation for students about what is to follow. It serves as an advanced organizer. Even if the lesson is a continuation from a previous lesson or a discovery activity, an overview should be given. Simply giving directions for an activity is not adequate for credit.

6. Uses motivating techniques to generate interest (2, 5, 8, 9)
The teacher uses a specific activity or instructional device to generate interest in the lesson. Stimulating techniques may include "attention getters," creative activities, unusual resources, thought-provoking questions, games, and simulations. The technique employed should be calculated to initiate, increase, or maintain student interest in the lesson.

7. Speaks in a manner that facilitates student learning (1, 4, 8, 9)
Considerations include volume, tone, characteristics, and speech mannerisms. The teacher's speech should encourage concentra-

tion on the lesson.

8. Structures the lesson in logical steps (1, 2, 4, 7, 9)
Explanations, descriptions, and activities are organized so that an orderly presentation is made. Examples include step-by-step approaches, explanations given in chronological order, concrete to abstract, or familiar to unfamiliar. Presentations considered may be given to the entire class or portions of the class.

9. Makes smooth transitions between activities (1, 2, 3, 8)
Connections between lesson segments are clear. Interruptions are handled with a minimum of class disruption. If students lose large amounts of instructional time (for example, time on task), the behavior is **not** demonstrated. (For example, students sitting idly waiting for others to finish.)

10. Uses personalized references for illustrations (1, 5, 8, 9)
The teacher expresses the relationship of the idea to an individual as an instructional example. Teachers may characterize a personal incident of the students and show its relation to the lesson. An example may be, "Johnny, don't you have a dog like the one in the story?" Placing the student hypothetically in a specific context is another example.

11. Uses a variety of instructional activities during a single lesson (1, 5, 9)
A variety of teaching methods may include drill, lecture, demonstration, questioning, discovery, discussion, learning centers. An occasional question is not considered a questioning approach. If the teacher uses a combination approach for instruction, the behavior is demonstrated.

12. Summarizes the major points of the lesson (1, 5, 8)
The teacher concludes the lesson with a review of the key ideas

presented or discussed. This review may be provided in a direct fashion or solicited through prompting questions such as "what were the major points we covered today?" However it is accomplished, there is a clear "conclusion" to the lesson.

Active Involvement

13. *Provides all students an opportunity for active involvement (2, 5, 6, 7, 9)*
Experiences provide an opportunity for all students to become actively involved in the lesson in some way by moving, writing, or talking. A discussion should provide all students at least one opportunity to contribute or answer questions.

14. *Provides all students opportunity to practice new skills (2, 7, 9)*
Application and/or practice is used to reinforce a concept or skill. Practice or application should be provided for at least one of the objectives for the lesson. At least one opportunity for each student is provided.

15. *Asks varied and appropriate questions (2, 4, 5, 7, 8, 9)*
Questions include a range of levels (factual, organizational, interpretive, creative) and help students relate to the subject matter.

(*) 16. *Asks reflective questions that stimulate thinking (1, 2, 5, 6)*
The teacher asks questions that encourage students to think about their own thinking processes and describe how they reach conclusions or why they make the suggestions they do.

17. *Encourages students to express personal ideas, needs, or interests (2, 5, 9)*
The teacher promotes student involvement for opinions and by listening attentively to responses. The teacher does not respond to

any student comment by conveying ridicule and/or sarcasm either verbally or nonverbally.

(*) 18. Encourages responsibility by involving students in decision-making (1, 3, 5)

Whenever appropriate, the teacher encourages students to provide input regarding classroom procedures. The teacher also encourages students to monitor their own performance and evaluate their own actions. The teacher provides choices and alternatives enabling students to make selections most appropriate to them.

Monitoring

19. Monitors student performance to determine needs for clarification, assistance, or adjustment (2, 4, 5, 8, 9)

The teacher may ask questions, look at samples of student performance, or use other informal evaluation procedures during the lesson (not a pre-test or post-test). Monitoring may involve asking questions.

20. Addresses disruptions that interfere with student learning (2, 5, 8, 9)

Disruptions are handled in accordance with the severity or nature of the disruption. The teacher addresses each disruption in a manner that encourages academic learning time and is as unobtrusive as possible. For example, the teacher may walk over to "disrupters" or make a nonverbal gesture while continuing to lecture or question. In all responses to student disruptions, the teacher demonstrates sensitivity to the well-being of the disrupting student(s) while assuring that the rights of other students in the class are not being violated.

21. Responds to students with special problems (1, 4, 5, 7)

The teacher provides additional instruction for individual students who need it. Whenever a student or small group of students indicates lack of skill or understanding, the teacher provides additional instruction or alternative activities. If it is not feasible to give special assistance at the time, the teacher arranges to provide help as soon as possible.

22. *Adjusts presentations and activities in response to feedback from students (5, 7, 8, 9)*
The teacher alters instructional strategies. Reteaching, changing plans, and designing impromptu learning activities for remaining class time are examples of adjustments. The teacher alters instruction if students lose interest, fail to understand, become frustrated, or complete assignments early.

Feedback

23. *Provides students feedback on their progress and performance (2, 4, 5, 7, 8, 9)*
The teacher attempts to inform students of their accuracy or progress. Feedback may be verbal, nonverbal, or written but must address correct or incorrect responses on student performances. (For example, "that's right" or "try again.")

24. *Praises student performance and expresses appreciation to students (1, 2, 5)*
The teacher responds positively to students when they participate in class or perform in a desirable manner. Positive reinforcement may include praise and encouragement, either verbal or nonverbal.

25. *Demonstrates support when responding to student errors (5, 7)*
Constructive criticism is accompanied by encouragement. The teacher recognizes student's responses as worthwhile contribu-

tions in spite of "errors". (For example, "You have the right idea but I am not sure you are applying it correctly," or "If you could elaborate, maybe your answer would be clearer to us.")

26. *Gives reasons for actions, decisions and directions (1, 2, 9)*
When appropriate, gives reasons for actions. (For example, "The reason we are in groups today is that..." or "I'll be with you in a minute, but right now I'm working with..."

Personal Factors

27. *Shows enthusiasm for learning and teaching (1, 5, 9)*
The teacher demonstrates excitement, enjoyment, or animated involvement in learning. Evidence may include intense or dramatic expressions, movement, vocal inflections, or facial changes.

28. *Communicates purposes and meaning of the lesson (1, 2, 5, 8, 9)*
The teacher shows a relationship between the lesson and long-range goals or everyday life; or shows the importance of single concepts to the mastery of important dimensions of the subject.

(*) 29. *The teacher shares personal experiences with students (1, 5)*
The teacher occasionally makes references to his or her interests and experiences as they relate to the lesson. Personal anecdotes are used as illustrations.

30. *Models courtesy and respect for students (1, 5, 9)*
The teacher uses student names in a friendly and supportive way. Non-verbal behavior is also supportive.

31. *Maintains patience and poise (1, 5, 9)*
The teacher allows reasonable time for students to ask questions and complete assignments. When involved in potentially disruptive situations, the teacher keeps his or her composure and

encourages a calm atmosphere.

(*) 32. Talks with students about their out-of-class activities during non-instructional time (1, 5)
The teacher uses time before and after lessons as an opportunity to talk with students about their interests and activities, such as being a part of a club or being a participant in activities such as band, gymnastics or soccer.

*indicates items not referenced in teacher performance appraisal systems and perhaps not as likely to be associated with student achievement.

Sources

Amos, L. (1985). Professionally and personally inviting teacher practices as related to affective course outcome. Doctoral dissertation. University of North Carolina at Greensboro.

Barnes, S. (1981). *Synthesis of Selected Research on Teaching Findings.* Austin, TX: Research and Development Center Teacher Education.

Brophy, J. (1983). Classroom organization and management. *The Elementary School Journal, 83*(4).

Fisher, C. W., et al. (1978). *Teaching and learning in the elementary school: A summary of the beginning teacher evaluation study.* Study Report VII-1. San Francisco, CA: Far West Laboratory for Educational Research and Development.

Johnston, H. J. (1984). A synthesis of research findings on middle level education. In Lounsbury, J. (editor), *Perspectives in Middle School Education, 1964-1984,* Columbus, OH: National Middle School Association, 134-157.

Purkey, W. W., & Novak, J. M. (1984). *Inviting School Success.* Belmont, CA: Wadsworth.

Rosenshine, B. (1983). Teaching functions in instructional programs. *The Elementary School Journal, 83*(4).

Stuck, G. et al. (1985). *Teacher Performance Appraisal System.* Raleigh, NC: State Department of Public Instruction.

Stulac, J. F., et al. (1982). *Assessments of Performance in Teaching Observation*

Instrument. Columbia, SC: South Carolina Educator Improvement
Task Force.

Chapter 7

Invitational Leadership

By Dean Fink

Each year, for the past thirty years of my experience in education, commentators have declared that education is in the midst of unprecedented change. The rapidly accelerating pace of change, they argue, required new and dramatic adjustments by school personnel. Now as I enter the twilight of my career, what strikes me as remarkable is how little schools have changed from my first year in a rural school to the schools of the present. As Cuban (1990) has written, the "deep structures" of schools remain fundamentally unchanged. Students are still, in the words of Purkey and Novak (1984), "labelled, libeled, sorted and grouped" (pp. 11-13). Schools are divided into grades, tracks, subjects, and bureaucratic layers. Students are passed from grade to grade and then given a certificate at the end. Accomplishment is often defined in terms of hours in the classroom as opposed to learning. This is an industrial model which reflects a vanishing age. Why, when equally resistant work cultures have adapted to the demands of an information age, has education remained fundamentally unchanged?

Sarason (1990) answers in his *The Predictable Failure of Educa-*

tional Reform: "in education the mistakes in conception and action have been many, and almost all of them derive from an inability to comprehend the nature of the school system" (p. 27). Traditionally, school reform has focused on one aspect or another without looking at the school as a total system. It has ignored power relationships, and until recently failed to see schools as distinctive cultures. Fullan (1990) captures this idea when he says:

> Our attention in policy, practice, and research has shifted in recent years, away from preoccupation with single innovations toward more basic integrative and systematic reform. Changes in the culture of schools, in the roles and relationships of schools, districts, universities, and states, and in integrating teacher development, school improvement, leadership, and curriculum toward more engaging learning experiences for students and teachers dominate the current scene and will continue to do so for the rest of the decade. (p. 137)

A teacher of agricultural science in rural Pennsylvania explained the concept more simply. He compared a school to a spider's web. If you touch one part of the web, the movement reverberates throughout the entire structure. Educational reformers who forget or ignore this concept do so at their peril. The attractiveness of invitational education, as described in this book, is that it provides a philosophical and conceptual gestalt that allows leaders to address the entire school as a system.

It will be the purpose of this chapter, therefore, to examine change in educational settings, and to suggest reasons why change has tended to be superficial and leave the "deep structures" of schooling unscathed. In addition, it will suggest how an invitational approach to leadership can effect profound changes that will enrich the lives of children.

The state insignia for New Mexico is based upon a Native American concept of the power of "four." The center of the insignia is the Sun, surrounded by symbolic representation of the four seasons, the four winds, the four directions, and the four ages of man. To supporters of invitational education, the four pillars provide guidance in their quest to make schools more responsive to the needs of students. The four pillars of invitational education allow invitational leaders to:

- ◆ invite themselves personally,
- ◆ invite themselves professionally,
- ◆ invite others personally,
- ◆ invite others professionally.

These four pillars provide the structure upon which an invitational school can be built. If a school is to become the inviting, welcoming place this book advocates, it must be led by leaders who structure their leadership upon these four pillars.

Inviting Yourself Personally: The First Pillar

Invitational leaders are proactive. They invite themselves personally by making choices; they make things happen, as opposed to letting things happen, or asking, what happened? In *The Empowered Manager*, Block (1987) challenges leaders to choose between caution and courage, maintenance and greatness, dependence and autonomy. When challenged to defend disinviting practices, educators often fall back on the argument that they have no choice. They contend that the amorphous **they** made us do it. They could be the superintendent, the parents, the state or provincial department of education. We seldom stop to ask, do we **really** have to do this?

What distinguishes humans from the animals is that, between stimulus and response, humankind has choices. Sometimes one must be prepared to live with negative consequences of choices. Even in the most dire circumstances, one always has choices. Viktor Frankl (1984) was a Jewish doctor who, unlike most of his family, survived a Nazi concentration camp. In his powerful book, *Man's Search for Meaning*, he tells of people who gave their last morsel of bread so that others might survive and they, too, survived, whereas others gave up on themselves and others and died very quickly. He wrote:

> The experiences of camp life show that [a person] does have a choice of action....[A person] can preserve a vestige of spiritual freedom, of independence of mind, even in such terrible conditions of psychic and physical stress....everything can be taken from a [person] but one thing: the last of the human freedoms—to choose one's attitude in any given set of circumstances, to choose one's own way. (p. 86).

Invitational leaders choose to invite others to approach the people, programs, policies, processes, and places in their school and school district from an invitational stance. It is a stance which on occasion requires courage and perseverance.

Invitational leaders begin with "the end in mind" (Covey, 1989, p. 95). Invitational leaders dream dreams; they have a vision of the way schools should be. All things are created twice, first in the mind, then in the doing. Block (1987) describes a vision as "a dream created in our waking hours of how we would like the organization to be." (p. 107)

Our collective perception of visionary leaders, however, raises images of the great visionary leaders like Martin Luther King or Winston Churchill. These were leaders whose charismatic qualities and the urgency of events that surrounded them led their followers through difficult times and towards a dream of a better future. Few of us in education are blessed with such charismatic qualities or are able to stir our supporters through the eloquence of our oratory. In spite of editorial excesses about the dire state of our schools, few of us could muster support by proclaiming a crisis in our schools. Schools do cry out for visionary, dynamic leadership to take them to the 21st century. We do need to dream dreams. What will your school or district look like in the year 2020? What structures will have to change or disappear to realize your vision?

The cynic might say, "Why bother dreaming dreams? Nothing substantive in education can change?" When one considers the dynamic events around us, even education can be dramatically changed. Who would have thought on January 1, 1989, that the entire map of Europe would be redrawn, the Berlin wall would become a money maker for entrepreneurs, and the Soviet Union would disintegrate?

Visions which become reality are the result of purposeful leaders who have challenged the accepted paradigm, invited themselves personally by choosing to pursue a dream. This idea was captured by Ted Kennedy at the funeral of Robert Kennedy, when he quoted his brother's words, "Some men see things as they are and say why, I dream of things that never were and say why not."

Inviting Yourself Professionally: The Second Pillar

Developing and committing oneself to a vision of a better way of doing things is important, but insufficient in itself to make a difference. By inviting oneself professionally, however, invitational leaders ensure that they have the competence and credibility to formulate and effect their vision of a new paradigm for their schools or districts.

Recent literature on leadership has tended to categorize leaders as people who do right things and managers as people who do things right. In the comparison, the management function tends to be seen as dull, routine, and definitely of secondary importance. Louis and Miles (1990) found that successful leaders were accomplished in both dimensions. Invitational leaders, therefore, not only establish a vision and invite people to share in the adventure, but they also acquire the expertise in problem-solving, decision-making, conflict resolution, and the creation of systems that enables the dream to be realized. Invitational leaders also invite themselves professionally by reading, relating, reflecting, and researching.

Invitational leaders construct this second pillar by keeping current through reading contemporary books and journals. Time is always the inhibitor, but a careful regimen of a few minutes a day can enhance the power of ideas immensely. The quality and quantity of educational research has escalated dramatically in the last ten years. Just as institutions need to grow and change, if you personally are not getting better and growing as a professional, you are getting worse. The well known Peter Principle postulates that you rise to your level of incompetence. Its corollary, Paul's Principle, contends that if you were competent at one point in your career, and you have failed to keep abreast of the changing nature of your job, then you have become increasingly incompetent. Unfortunately, education like most professions, has people with 20 years of experience which is in reality one year of experience repeated 20 times.

We learn best from our peers. Invitational leaders build networks through their attendance at conferences and workshops, writing to colleagues, and joining organizations such as the International Alliance for Invitational Education. Teachers' federations, principals' associations, and curriculum councils are also useful avenues to make the kind of contacts which contribute to the enhancement of our professional competence.

Reflective practice as popularized by Schon (1987) and others is also a vital part of inviting oneself professionally. Reflection is the practice or art of analyzing our actions, decisions, or products by focusing on our process of achieving them. The following questions capture the essence of the reflective practitioner. "What do I do?" is reflection on action. "What does this mean?" gets at the principles behind the action. "How did I come to be this way?"

forces individuals to confront their own paradigms or mind maps (Senge, 1990). "How might I do this differently?" is reflection for action in that it examines the results of practices (Smyth, 1989). To invite oneself professionally, the leader needs to answer these questions in a rigorous way. What quantitative and qualitative data can be examined to respond to these questions? What do colleagues, teachers, students, and parents say about your performance? What do the parents think of your school? What instruments do you use to collect data?

A derivative, but more in-depth form of reflection, is research. Few teachers and principals actually undertake small scale research projects in their school or classroom, but this is a useful way to direct or redirect practice. Hopkins (1988) contends that:

> Classroom research generates hypotheses about teaching, and encourages teachers to use this research to make their teaching more competent.... Undertaking research in their own classrooms is one way in which teachers can take increased responsibility for their actions and create a more energetic and dynamic environment in which teaching and learning can occur. (pp. 1-2)

If one takes this notion and applies it to the larger context of the school, then one gets the essence of how the invitational leader uses action research as a useful tool to invite oneself professionally. Hopkins' book is a useful beginning point for educators interested in undertaking action research in their school or classroom.

Inviting Others Personally: The Third Pillar

Invitational leaders not only invite themselves personally and professionally, but they also invite others personally and professionally. The third pillar of invitational leadership, inviting others personally, requires leaders who not only have vision, but also voice. In her book, *The Female Advantage*, Helgesen (1991) writes of replacing the concept of vision with the concept of voice. She contends that vision is a one way-process. As a vision, it may exist alone in the mind of a single human being, but a voice requires someone to hear it. Voice, therefore, is interactive. The metaphor becomes more accurate if one considers vision as the ability to look into the distance and determine an appropriate path. Without the concept of voice, however, it becomes a solitary trip. Invitational leaders possess both a vision and voice.

Vision and voice come from one's personal stance. If you think of those occasions when you worked for someone else, or remember the first day of school when you met your new teachers, unconsciously you had a set of questions in your mind directed at those people who had power over your life. Some of these questions might have been: What kind of person are you? Can I trust you? Do you know where you are going? Am I invited to join you on the journey? How much do you understand me and genuinely care? Do you respect me as an individual? How committed are you to the vision? Is there intentionality to your words and behavior?

People whose followership you need ask similar types of questions. The way you as the leader behave towards them is based upon your stance. The inviting stance of trust, respect, optimism, and intentionality provides the basis for personal invitations to others. Many people have authority, but few have power. Power only comes from others' willingness to follow your leadership.

The leader who operates from this invitational stance and invites others personally must behave politically. It may even be argued that one's ability to invite in the other dimensions of people, policies, programs, processes, and places is dependent on the leader's ability to behave politically. James McGregor Burns (1978) defines acting in a political way as "exchanging gratifications in a political market place" (p. 258). You scratch my back, I scratch yours. To act politically, however, is to behave in an ethical, democratic way; to raise the aspirations of others through teaching, mentoring, and coaching. The means are those of "honesty, responsibility, fairness, the honoring of commitment" (Burns, 1978, p. 425) Acting politically means building collaborative cultures through shared vision and shared decision-making. It means doing **with** people as opposed **to** doing to people. It means operating from an invitational stance of trust, optimism, respect, and intentionality. It also means you know how to effect authentic change within complex organizations.

Burns describes leaders who behave politically as transformational leaders. This concept has been developed in the educational literature by Sergiovanni (1990) and Leithwood (1992). They suggest, however, that ethical political behavior is necessary for the ongoing management of schools. This style, described by Leithwood as transactional leadership, "is based on an exchange of services...for various kinds of rewards... that the leader controls at least in part" (p. 9). He further reports that transactional leadership practices, some claim, "help people recognize what needs to be done in order to reach a desired outcome and also may increase their confidence and motivation" (p. 9). Transactional leadership practices are necessary for getting the day to day business done, but transformational approaches are necessary to effect positive change.

Invitational leaders blend the two styles by creating trust, not only in their leadership, but also in the systems which they put into place. Traditionally, change efforts have been predicated on changing peoples' attitudes as a prerequisite to behavior change. There is considerable evidence that such an approach is self-defeating (Fullan, 1991; Louis & Miles, 1990). Unless people get involved and muck around in a new process, or at least see colleagues involved, change will not occur. Similarly, if one waits to initiate change until everyone on a school staff has agreed, it could be a long wait.

Two solutions are ad hoc committees and pilot projects. Rather than establishing permanent structures for change, people who think politically start with an ad hoc group of staff who are willing to experiment; the more broadly representative of the various subcultures of a school the better. Let this group pilot the innovation. Provide them with support, profile, and rigorous evaluation. As others show interest, let them get involved to the extent they are willing to be involved. Let participants know that not everything will be a success. When things go off the rails, be there to help the person try again. Proponents of invitational education know the importance of "I can" for students. This principle is as important, if not more important, with adults who have spent many years building defences for their self-concepts.

Inviting Others Professionally: The Fourth Pillar

If we as leaders are to avoid "the predictable failure of educational reform" (Sarason, 1990), then the challenge is to channel the energies of various stakeholder groups into productive activities for students. Inviting oneself and others personally and inviting oneself professionally are, therefore, only prerequisites for the ultimate leadership challenge, the fourth pillar of invitational leadership, inviting others professionally.

Professionally inviting leaders look at the big picture and articulate aspirations, while sweating the small stuff. Louis and Miles (1990), in their study of change in secondary schools, described the politically adept leader as one who uses every opportunity to discuss values, to articulate a vision, and to place each issue into the context of the larger picture. Without attending to small but irritating management issues, the big issues become obscured. As one develops a discipline code, it is placed in the larger context of the invitational school. When a staff organizes a parents' night, it is done so within the context of how can we invite parents. It is through this slow but necessary process that people begin to share the vision, and it in turn gives meaning to changes within the school. "If reforms are to be successful, individuals and groups must find meaning concerning what should change as well as how to go about it" (Fullan, 1991, p. xi).

Another necessary strategy for inviting others professionally is to promote a collaborative school or district culture. This is not a new idea. Dewey (1937) many years ago said, "Teachers need to be in contact with one another so they may pool their shared ideas relative to methods and results: to deny this cooperative effort is to promote waste" (p. 462). Rosenholtz (1989) expressed the idea in more contemporary terms when she said "...the extent of school goal-setting, evaluation, shared values and collaboration represent the workplace conditions most conducive to teachers' learning opportunities and their schools' self-renewal" (p. 79).

Similarly, Kanter (1984), in her examination of change in complex organizations, argues for greater collaboration in the workplace when she says: "...corporate entrepreneurs produce innovative achievement by working in collaborative/participative fashion: persuading much more than ordering" (p. 237). She contends that successful organizational leaders, regardless of whether they are in the private or public sectors, need to be skilled at team-building, seeking input from others, showing political sensitivity to the interests of others, and possessing a willingness to share rewards and recognition.

Unfortunately, the existing paradigm of relationships in many schools is one of teacher isolation. As Little (1988) states, "Traditional authority relations in schools and districts, as well as conventional teacher evaluation procedures, communicate a view of teaching as an individual enterprise" (p. 84). In a similar vein, Hargreaves (1989) reports, "If isolation purges the classroom of blame and criticism it also shuts out possible sources of praise and support" (p. 7).

According to Rosenholtz (1989), there are moving schools and stuck schools. A moving school is one in which instructional goals are shared goals, and the norms of the culture are those of collaboration, continuous improvement, and optimism that all students can learn. Stuck schools are characterized by little staff attachment to school-wide goals and norms of self-reliance and intellectual poverty. In a stuck school there is a "numbing sameness." Teachers behave like victims and go about their business with a degree of fatalism. In moving schools, there is freedom to try, fail, risk, innovate, ask for help, and learn. In stuck schools teachers try to exercise freedom from parents, principals, consultants, new ideas, risk, and change.

While a major difference between moving and stuck schools is collaboration, it alone is not a panacea for all the ills of schools. Collaboration can exist in disinviting ways. As a colleague has pointed out, "Hells Angels are collegial." An important key to invitational leadership is the ability to invite colleagues both personally and professionally to develop a culture which promotes norms of both collaboration and continuous improvement.

One of the greatest impediments to collaboration, however, is decision making within the school. Simply stated, who makes what decisions? Debates in the literature advocate various types of decision-making styles for leaders. The school reality, however, suggests that one style cannot account for all the types of decisions made in a school. A question of child abuse is not one for staff discussion, whereas a selection of textbooks may very well be left totally to teachers. An approach which teachers appreciate and which recognizes this dilemma is for a school staff to establish a decision-making matrix. One part of the matrix lists all the types of decisions to be made in a school. The other part of the matrix indicates who initiates the need for a decision, who has input into the decision, who makes the decision, who is informed of the decision, and who is responsible for implementing the decision. Such a discussion eliminates ambiguity and facilitates genuine collaboration and continuous improvement.

Historically, when reforms failed to produce the improvement proponents expected, the ritual search for villains began. Invariably, reformers, external to schools, pointed their fingers at intransigent administrators and reactive teachers. Consider, for instance, the traditional way to effect change. Policy-makers legislate a change, conduct the usual information giving sessions, and then try to ensure that the innovation "takes" by initiating elaborate monitoring and control systems. These systems can be as simple as requiring teachers to adhere religiously to a manual, or as elaborate as dictating textbook content and approaches or initiating a testing system designed to drive the curriculum. As Sarason (1990) writes, however, "Any educational reform that does not explicitly and courageously own up to issues surrounding changing patterns of power relationships is likely to fail" (p. 31).

The invitational leader, therefore, sees teachers as knowledge workers, professional educators, and leaders, not workers whose mandate is to implement someone else's solution to classroom issues. Stenhouse (1984) captures this idea very well when he states:

> Good teachers are necessarily autonomous in professional judgement. They do not need to be told what to do. They are not professionally the dependents of researchers, of superintendents, of innovators or supervisors. This does not mean that they do not welcome access to ideas created by other people at other places or in other times. Nor do they reject advice, consultancy or support. But they do know that ideas and people are not of much real use until they are digested to the point where they are subject to the teacher's own judgement. In short, it is the task of all educationalists outside the classroom to serve the teachers; for only teachers are in position to create good teaching. (p. 69)

If, as Fullan (1991) says, "change in education depends on what teachers do or think—it's as simple and complex as that" (p. 117), then how does the invitational leader promote the commitment and involvement required to work towards a shared vision? One important answer is a carefully planned staff development program. Effective staff development is based on adult learning principles and the belief that teachers are able, responsible, and worthwhile, and want to improve in order to be more effective for their students.

Joyce's (1990) principles of theory, demonstration, practice, feedback, and coaching have proven useful in developing teacher efficacy (Fullan, 1991; Louis & Miles, 1990). The disinviting aspect of this model, however, is that it is still a doing **to** as opposed to a doing **with**. As Hargreaves and Dawe (1989) argue, most in-service programs:

> ...withhold from teachers opportunities for wider reflection about the context of their work, which deprofessionalize and disempower teachers in denying them the opportunity to discuss and debate what and how they teach; which smuggle bureaucratically determined ends into ostensibly neutral procedures for improving technical skills. (p. 27.)

Teachers require the time to discuss, contemplate, and investigate how a suggested innovation has meaning for them. They also need opportunities to experiment, as well as the support to sustain innovation.

Since the very clear trend, world-wide, is to effect change school by school by school, the best in-service climate is to ensure that each school is a learning community for teachers and its principal. In Barth's (1990) words, the principal becomes the "head learner." Staff development in such environments becomes part of the ongoing life of the school, and is intimately related to its goals. Change occurs through leaders who can invite others personally and professionally to create a learning community within a school. Schools and school systems, therefore, will thrive to the degree that learning equals or exceeds the pace of change.

How does one create such a learning community when the

situation is quite the opposite? The important point is to start someplace. This may sound like rather simplistic advice, but in reality if you wait until everyone agrees with a new direction, it could be a long wait. There will inevitably be people reluctant to participate. What then? Block (1987) suggests analyzing your colleagues' willingness to buy in to your invitational vision on two dimensions: how well people trust you, and to what extent people agree with you. Those who both trust you and agree with you must continue to be invited in order to maintain the direction. Those who trust you but question the vision or the changes it implies are your most valuable colleagues because they will give you honest feedback. It is through interaction with this group that one gradually begins to build a shared vision. To deal with groups or individuals who don't trust you, or who disagree with you, or both, you must continue to invite through seeking to build trust, listening for understanding, and providing information and opportunities to participate. In the last analysis, however, a collaborative culture will not sustain those who are intentionally disinviting. As my colleague Terry Parry says, "don't water the rocks."

When there is a fairly clear indication that the staff is working in a collaborative fashion and there tends to be agreement on the directions for the school, it is useful for the staff to articulate a mission, philosophy, or a credo. A mission statement answers two questions: what business are we in, and how do we do business. It should be the articulation of the organization's shared vision. A mission statement is the product of the long, sometimes tedious process of clarifying values and shaping a vision for the organization. It should not be rushed. What separates a true mission statement from pure rhetoric is the degree of commitment from the people in the organization. The central focus for goal setting, problem solving, and conflict resolution is the mission. Here is one example of a mission statement:

> The staff members of the Four Pillars High School
> commit themselves to:

◆ teaching for learning for all students (Lezotte, 1990)
◆ preparing students for an information age.
The staff members of the Four Pillars High School will do so by:
◆ ensuring that the school's staff applies the principles of invitational education,
◆ developing a learning community for students, staff, and the community.

Teachers, administrators, and school board members often feel overwhelmed by the number and rapidity of change efforts. As a result, the tendency is to try to do everything and accomplish nothing. A next important step to invite others professionally, therefore, is to develop a school growth plan based upon the mission. A school growth plan is a strategic plan which is driven by vision, values, and goals. Traditional long-range planning focused upon dividing up turf and getting things done efficiently. A school growth plan commits the school to a few "high leverage" objectives for an extended period of time. The major challenge within such strategic planning, however, is to determine what high leverage objectives to pursue.

Senge (1990) explains that if you place a frog in boiling water, it will immediately jump out. If, however, you place that frog in lukewarm water and gradually raise the temperature to the boiling point, the frog will gradually adapt until it becomes groggier and groggier and unable to jump out of the pot. Even though there are no restraints, the frog will sit in the water and boil to death. If we are to plan strategically, then we have to be able to determine when and how the temperature is being turned up. One answer is what Waterman (1988) calls "friendly facts." These are data which decision makers can use to reflect on practice and make informed decisions. Can you answer such questions as: Are the students learning? Are they learning things that are important and significant? Is your student population changing? Is society getting its money's worth? Are your teachers growing and developing professionally? Is your school an effective school? Is it effective for all students? Is your school an invitational school? These are tough questions, but if the leader is not prepared to address them, then others have ready-made answers which will be detrimental to students.

In the pursuit of "friendly facts," invitational leaders invite teachers, students, parents, and community members to participate in the process. Many a good plan has failed because of a lack of community support or the leader's failure to read the community accurately. School board members, for instance, are an important source of community information and potential support.

Being a school board member is often a no-win job. The public sees board members as spendthrifts; the educators liken them to "Scrooge." Most school board members are genuinely concerned about the quality of education for all students. Unfortunately, we only hear about the more political types. The processes of developing shared visions, missions, and goals should not exclude the people who put up their hands at school board meetings. Invitational leaders invite elected officials to share in the aspirations for the school.

In summary, a school growth plan is a small list of priorities or areas of emphasis, which the school commits itself to develop over at least a three-year period. The specific number of areas will depend on the size of the school. The process of developing a school growth plan is a collaborative one which involves an entire school staff. It reflects a common mission that captures the shared values and beliefs of the teachers.

There are a number of useful planning models which incorporate the basic principles described. *An Action Guide To School Improvement* (Loucks-Horsley and Hergert, 1985), *Workbook for School Improvement* (Lezotte, 1990), and *Building A School Growth Plan* (Halton Board, 1989) all provide excellent models for school planning. Effective school growth planning is an investment in the future by the entire staff, not just the leader. The process, however, is only as good as the leadership provided and the degree of collaboration and staff leadership promoted by the leader.

At the center of the insignia of New Mexico, referred to in the introduction to this chapter, is the Sun. To stretch the metaphor to encompass invitational leadership, the leader, like the Sun, provides the unity, promotes the warmth which nurtures relationships, and allows individuals to flourish within a collaborative culture. Like the Sun, the leader influences pervasively throughout the organization. In an invitational organization, the climate created by the leader allows individuals to flourish both personally and professionally.

The Sun fits within a highly complex and interrelated solar system. To understand it, scientists must see the interconnectedness of the myriad of components of the solar system. While human organizations are not that complex or daunting, they certainly seem to be to those involved. Leaders who understand that schools are complex organizations and apply this insight to the invitations they extend to themselves and others personally and professionally will enable schools and their students to move into the 21st century with wisdom, confidence, and joy.

References

Barker, J. (1989). *Discovering the future*. St. Paul, MN: I.L.I. Press.

Barth, W. (1990). *Improving schools from within*. San Francisco, CA: Jossey Bass.

Bennis, W., & Nanus, B (1985). *Leaders*. New York: Harper and Row.

Block, P. (1987). *The empowered manager*. San Francisco, CA: Jossey Bass.

Burns, J. M. (1978). *Leadership*. New York: Harper Torch Books.

Halton Board of Education (1989). *Building a school growth plan*. Burlington, Ontario: Halton Board.

Covey, S. (1989). *The 7 habits of highly effective people*. Toronto, Ontario: Simon and Schuster.

Cuban, L (1990). Reforming again, again, and again. *Educational Re-*

searcher, 19(1), 3-13.

Dewey, J. (1937). Democracy and educational administration. *School and Society, 45*(6), 9-10.

Frankl, V. (1984). *Man's search for meaning.* Toronto, Ontario: Pocket Books.

Fullan, M. (1991). *The new meaning of educational change.* Toronto, Ontario: O.I.S.E. Press.

Fullan, M. (1990). Beyond implementation. *Curriculum Implementation, 20*(2), 137-139.

Hargreaves, A., & Dawe, R (1989). Coaching as unreflective practice: Contrived collegiality or collaborative culture. Paper presented at the American Educational Research Association, San Francisco, CA.

Hargreaves, A. (1990). Cultures of teaching. *OPSTF News,* February, 5-10.

Helgesen, K. (1991). *The female advantage.* New York: Doubleday.

Hopkins, D. (1988). *A teachers guide to classroom research.* Philadelphia, PA: Open University Press.

Joyce, B. (editor). (1990). *Changing school culture through staff development.* Alexandria, VA: Association for Supervision and Curriculum Development.

Kanter, J. M. (1983). *The change masters.* New York: Simon and Schuster.

Kouzis, J. M., & Posner, B. Z. (1987). *The leadership challenge.* San Francisco, CA: Jossey-Bass.

Lezotte, L. (1990). Dear colleague letter. *Effective Schools Abstracts,* January.

Lezotte, L. (1990). *Workbook for developing a district plan for school improvement.* Okemos, MI: Effective Schools Products.

Leithwood, K. (1992). The move toward transformational leadership. *Educational Leadership, 49*(5), 8-11.

Little, J. W. (1988). Assessing the prospects for teacher leadership. In *building a professional culture in schools.* New York: Columbia University.

Louis, K., & Miles, M. (1990). *Improving the urban high school: What works and why.* New York: Teachers College Press.

Maxcy, S. J. (1991). *Educational leadership: A critical pragmatic perspective.* New York: Bergin & Garvey.

Naisbett, J (1990). *Megatrends 2000.* New York: William Morrow and Company.

Purkey, W. W., & Novak, J. M. (1984). *Inviting school success.* Belmont, CA:

Wadsworth Press.

Rosenholtz, S. J.(1989). *Teacher workplace.* New York: Longmans.

Sarason, S. (1990). *The predictable failure of educational reform.* San Francisco, CA: Jossey Bass.

Schon, D. (1987). *Educating the reflective practitioner.* San Francisco, CA: Jossey Bass.

Senge, P. (1990). *The fifth discipline.* Toronto, Ontario: Doubleday.

Sergiovanni, T. J. (1990). Adding value to leadership gets extraordinary results. *Educational Leadership, 47*(8), 23-27.

Smith, W., & Andrews, R. (1989). *Instructional leadership.* Alexandria, VA: Association for Supervision and Curriculum Development.

Smyth, J. (1989). Developing and sustaining critical reflection in teacher education. *Journal of Teacher Education, 40*(2), 2-9.

Stenhouse, L. (1984). Artistry and teaching: The teacher as focus of research and development. In Hopkins, D., and Wideen, M. (editors), *Alternative perspectives on school improvement.* Lewes, England: Falmer Press.

Waterman, R. (1989). *The renewal factor.* New York: Bantam Books.

Wolf, D., *et.al.* (1991). To use their minds well: Investigating new forms of student assessment. In Grant, G. (editor), *Review of research in education.* Washington, DC: American Educational Research Association.

Implications
for Higher Education

Chapter 8

An Analysis of Adult Cognitive-Developmental Theory and Invitational Education

By Dorothy S. Russell

While adult developmental theory and invitational theory are rooted in different philosophical orientations, in practice they share more commonalities than differences. Adult developmental theory has its roots in John Dewey's progressive philosophy and cognitive-developmental psychology, while invitational theory stems from a romantic/humanistic philosophy and perceptual psychology. However, both share and are shaped by the common assumption that individuals continue to grow and develop throughout their lifetimes. Both assume untapped human potential.

Purkey and Novak (1984) state that "invitational education is the process by which people are cordially summoned to realize their relatively boundless potential" (p. 3). In like manner, adult developmental theorists deny that adulthood is a period of stagnation or worse yet degeneration. They posit that adults can learn new abilities as well as improve old abilities (Sprinthall & Theis-Sprinthall, 1983). Thus, both theories are optimistic in their view of the elasticity of the human mind.

The purpose of this essay is to examine the similarities and differences between adult cognitive-developmental theory and invitational theory. To accomplish this goal, a brief review of invitational theory and adult cognitive-developmental theory will be necessary. Further, the writer will suggest that the practice of invitational theory can be strengthened by adoption of the "constructive mismatch," a concept at the core of adult developmental theory.

Invitational Theory

Invitational education (Purkey & Novak, 1984) is a theory of educational practice that assumes people have untapped potential in all areas of human development and that people are able, valuable, responsible, and worthy of respect. Invitations are at the heart of this theory. Invitations are messages which communicate to people that they are valuable, able, responsible, and worthy of respect. Schools or educational environments (places) can be designed to promote the development of individuals through inviting programs, policies, processes, and people.

Invitational theory is grounded in perceptual psychology and self concept theory. Thus, people behave in keeping with how they perceive themselves and the world around them. How we view ourselves (self-concept) influences everything we do and think. Individuals form their self-concepts through interactions with significant others, i.e., parents, teachers, and peers. Self-concept is the sum of all invitations/disinvitations sent and received:

> Let people realize clearly that every time they
> threaten someone or humiliate or hurt unneces-
> sarily or dominate or reject another human being,
> they become forces for the creation of psychopa-
> thology, even if these be small forces. Let them
> recognize that every man [sic] who is kind, help-
> ful, decent, psychologically democratic, affection-
> ate, and warm, is a psychotherapeutic force even

though a small one. (Maslow, 1970, p. 254)

People function at one of four levels: intentionally disinviting, unintentionally disinviting, unintentionally inviting, and intentionally inviting. The goal is to consistently function at the intentionally inviting level, thus becoming Maslow's therapeutic force for good.

Intentionality is a key concept in invitational theory. The individual who is unintentionally inviting is unaware of his/her behavior, therefore unlikely to repeat the behavior. Intentionality also signifies commitment. The inviting educator intentionally adopts a teaching strategy or program of study that will promote positive student self-concepts.

Each of us is continually in the process of sending messages (invitations) to ourselves and others. These messages can take the form of personal messages, "I look great today," "You look great today," or professional messages, "My class went well today," "Your class went well today." Inviting educators are urged to invite themselves as well as others in order to promote their own development.

Adult Cognitive-Developmental Theory

A key assumption of adult developmental theory is that adults can continue to grow and develop in cognitive complexity and interpersonal maturity. Growth does not signify merely new learning, but a structural change in the way the individual processes knowledge and justifies beliefs. Evidence for adult development is found in the work of Hunt (1971), Perry (1970), Kohlberg (1979), and Kitchener and King (1990), as well as others.

There is no all-encompassing model of adult development. Instead, theorists have isolated aspects of behavior, such as cognitive (Piaget, 1963), moral (Kohlberg, 1969), and ego (Loevinger, 1976). For example, Hunt, Perry, Kitchener, and King have studied development in terms of epistemology, i.e., how does one know, learn, and justify one's beliefs. Hunt (1971) suggests four stages of increasing conceptual complexity and interpersonal maturity. Perry's (1970) research examined the development of intellectual reasoning and ethical behavior in college students. Perry identified nine stages through which students progress. Kitchener and King (1990) have developed a seven stage model of reflective judgement which examines individuals' assumptions about knowledge and the way they justify their beliefs or decisions.

Stage models are at the center of cognitive-developmental theory. One must be able to visualize the later phases of development to know how to guide the individual through the present stage. Dewey (1902) supplies the rationale for developmental stages:

> Of what use, educationally speaking, is it to be able to see the end in the beginning? How does it assist us in dealing with the early stages of growth to be able to anticipate its later phases? To see the outcome is to know in what direction the present experience is moving, provided it moves normally and soundly. The far-away point, which is of no significance to us simply as far away, becomes of huge importance the moment we take it as defining a present direction of movement. (pp. 12-13)

In developmental psychology, it is generally agreed that stages share the following characteristics:

> 1. Each stage implies a distinct way of thinking (cognitive structure) that is qualitatively different from the stages both preceding and following.
> 2. Persons progress through these stages in invariant order, i.e., through the first stage, then the second, etc. There is no skipping around.
> 3. Later stages are more complex and desirable than earlier stages.

4. Movement through the stages is not automatic. Movement occurs as a result of the interaction between the individual and the environment.

At the heart of developmental theory is the understanding that development occurs not by maturation alone, nor by direct learning, but by a series of interactions between the person and the environment. "Cognitive development, which is defined as change in cognitive structures, is assumed to depend upon experience" (Kohlberg & Mayer, 1972, p. 457).

Sprinthall and Theis-Sprinthall (1983) suggest the following guidelines for promoting development:

1. Development appears to be influenced by placing individuals in significant role-taking experiences. Examples might be student teaching or taking on a new position with increased responsibilities.

2. Experience must be balanced by careful and continual guided reflection.

3. Efforts to promote development should be continuous over time. Developmental growth is slow and not likely to produce measurable change for at least a year.

4. Since development implies movement towards new modes of thought and problem solving, there is a loss of the old and familiar. Persons need considerable support to grow into new behaviors.

5. To move individuals towards new modes of thought and behavior, dissonance or conflict must be introduced. The constructive mismatch is the intentional manipulation of the environment so that the individual is forced to examine or confront the conflict between old and new beliefs.

Similarities

The most significant commonality between adult cognitive-developmental theory and invitational theory is their optimistic stance for the individual's continuous growth and development. The opening quotation in Purkey and Novak's book (1984) is a quote from Sidney Jourard (1968) which states: "I now believe there is no biological, geographical, social, economic, or psychological determiner of man's [sic] condition that he cannot transcend if he is suitably invited or challenged to do so" (p. 58.

Both Hunt (1971) and Theis-Sprinthall (1984) report modest gains in adult conceptual level after varying educational treatments. Their assumption is that persons of low conceptual level will need high structure during learning while persons of high conceptual level would prefer low structure. Their research supports this hypothesis. Sprinthall and Theis-Sprinthall (1987) recommend designing teacher education programs and in-service programs for teachers in such a way that cognitive-development can be promoted.

Both adult cognitive-developmental theory and invitational theory emphasize the role of the environment in the growth process. They are both concerned with interactions between the individual and the environment. Invitational theory recognizes the importance of messages sent by others in the development of one's own self-concept and world view. Invitational theory goes beyond personal messages to recognize the importance of all aspects of the environment. Purkey and Novak (1984) state:

> Just as everyone and everything in hospitals should encourage healing, everyone and everything in schools should invite the realization of human potential. This involves the **people** (teachers, bus drivers, aides, cafeteria staff, secretaries, librarians, nurses, counselors, custodians, crossing

> guards, administrators, the **places** (classrooms, offices, hallways, commons, restrooms, playing fields, gymnasiums, libraries), the **policies** (rules, codes, procedures), and the **programs** (curricular or extracurricular). (p. 2).

In invitational theory, the environment is important in the sense that an inviting environment supplies the individual with the support (emotional, social, academic) necessary for growth.

In like manner, developmental psychology recognizes the individual as the constructor of knowledge as a result of interaction with things, people, and ideas in the environment. "For the interactionist, experience is essential to stage progression, and more or richer stimulation leads to faster advance though the stages" (Kohlberg & Mayer, 1972, p. 459). As we have noted above, two key conditions for growth appear to be significant role-taking experience and the constructive mismatch.

For the developmentalist, the environment must supply both support and challenge—the constructive mismatch. Support is necessary as the individual encounters new ideas and responsibilities and must give up old ways of thinking and doing. However, for the developmentalist, the added ingredient is the constructive mismatch. "The hypothesis is that some moderate or optimal degree of conflict or discrepancy constitutes the most effective experience for structural change" (Kohlberg & Mayer, 1972, p. 459).

In the classroom, the constructive mismatch may be encouraged through the dilemma-discussion approach. In this approach, a moral dilemma is introduced and students are invited to share their views. For example, "What should a district attorney do when she has clear evidence that a murderer did perpetrate the crime; yet, that evidence is inadmissible in a court of law?" This approach to instruction requires the teacher to be both a facilitator of discussion and a skillful poser of questions. Research demonstrates that students understand and prefer reasoning on a stage

(Kohlberg) one step higher than their modal stage. Over a period of time, this kind of classroom discussion can have an impact on a student's level of moral maturity (Sprinthall & Sprinthall, 1987).

An example of the constructive mismatch in teacher education is requiring prospective teachers to tutor "high risk" minority children in an urban school. In this instance, the dissonance is produced by working with children from backgrounds that are highly divergent from those of the prospective teachers. The experience is managed by the instructor, who guides both the students' work and their reflections upon the experience.

Purkey and Novak (1984) are very aware that to maintain an inviting stance one must take care of one's own needs as well. Inviting teachers need to personally and professionally invite themselves in order to sustain their own professional energy. As examples of professional self-invitations, they cite: graduate education, conference attendance, professional reading, participation in professional organizations, and research and writing for publication. In discussing self-invitations for professional growth, Purkey and Novak (1984) come close to suggesting that challenges are necessary as well as a supportive environment. Certainly, graduate programs and research and writing for publication are challenging!

Reflection is essential to the developmentalist. One of the conditions for promoting development is careful and continuous guided reflection upon experience. Experience by itself can be miseducative. For example, when students tutor inner city "high risk" students, it is essential that there is guided reflection. Left on their own, the experience may lead to reinforced stereotypes. In their book *Inviting School Success*, Purkey and Novak (1984) acknowledge Dewey's argument that reflection upon experience is essential for education. They recommend examining one's perceptions as a means of better understanding oneself and others. However, in practice, little emphasis appears to be placed upon reflection.

Finally, the belief in intentionality is important to both invitational theory and adult cognitive-developmental theory. In invitational education, the goal is to be consistently intentionally inviting. Adult development theorists firmly embrace the idea that the environment must be manipulated to ensure individuals the appropriate constructive mismatch, thus assuring intentionality.

Differences

There are two key differences between invitational theory and adult developmental theory—stage models and the constructive mismatch.

Developmentalists build stage models to describe age- and experience-related structural differences in behavior. As stated by Dewey, they believe the future provides insight and direction for the present. Depending upon the domain involved, the highest stages may represent formal operations (Piaget, 1963), cognitive complexity (Hunt, 1971), or principled moral reasoning (Kohlberg, 1979). Invitational theory does not concern itself with stages of development. Individuals are invited to realize their full potential. What that full potential means is never clearly articulated. However, based on this writer's understanding of invitational theory, Maslow's (1970) self actualization stage may most closely describe invitational theory's realization of full human potential.

Invitational theory does posit four levels of functioning: intentionally disinviting, unintentionally disinviting, unintentionally inviting, and intentionally inviting. However, these are not stages in the sense of invariant order. In fact, one could be both intentionally disinviting and intentionally inviting on the same day. No structural changes take place in going from one level to another; it is rather a matter of attitude and values.

Developmentalists recognize the need to create dissonance to stimulate growth. Piaget calls this process disequilibrium. "Disequilibrium, or imbalance, occurs when a person encounters an object or event that he is unable to assimilate due to the inadequacy of his cognitive structures" (Ginsburg & Opper, 1988, p. 227). Piaget recognizes that a moderately discrepant environment produces growth:

> In sum, disequilibrium, a major cause of cognitive development, is caused by disturbances, perturbations, or conflicts that occur when there is a discrepancy between the child's schemes, which determine what she is able to assimilate, and the requirements of certain experiences. (Ginsburg & Opper, 1988, p. 229)

Theis-Sprinthall (personal communication, January, 1991) uses the term "constructive mismatch" to signify that while the environment may be mismatched, and therefore produce anxiety to the individual, the end goal is constructive and growth producing.

Invitational theory suggests that the same environment, a warm, caring, and supportive environment, would be best for everyone. Developmental theory firmly believes that the individual must meet challenges to grow. In the invitational classroom, the student does grow because the teacher provides the support and the curriculum the challenge. Thus, differences appear subtle. As long as an individual receives support and challenge from the environment, growth is possible. The real difference is one of intentionality. The developmentalist assures that the individual will receive both support and challenge.

Conclusion

This essay has examined the similarities and differences between invitational theory and adult developmental theory. In practice, there are many commonalities. Both theories are optimistic with regard to human development. Both see adults in the process of becoming. Both recognize the need for supportive environments which convey positive regard.

The differences lie in stage theory and in the concept of the constructive mismatch. Given that the goal of invitational theory—the development of full human potential—is indefinite, a stage model appears unnecessary. However, the concept of the constructive mismatch could easily be integrated with invitational theory. The most inviting environment for learning could be both challenging and supportive.

The inviting teacher could be encouraged and taught to deliberately challenge students through the introduction of new and conflicting ideas, either through the dilemma-discussion approach or through the careful selection of curriculum materials. In addition, invitational teachers could be taught to recognize learning styles and to vary their instructional strategies accordingly. As noted previously, the gradual withdrawal of structure in the classroom has been shown to increase students' cognitive complexity. Also, the importance of role-taking to the educational process could be stressed in invitational education. Carefully-managed peer tutoring experiences have the potential to develop an understanding of the viewpoints of others. Finally, invitational education could place greater emphasis on the process of guided reflection.

The constructive mismatch assumes that there will be some discomfort in the process of development. The key is to provide support at the same time. Invitational theory is a theory of support. The goal of education for both the invitational educator and the developmentalist should be the newly-found pride and increasingly positive self-concept expressed by the words, "I can do it" or "I understand."

References

Dewey, J. (1902). The child and the curriculum. In *The school and the society*. Chicago, IL: University of Chicago Press.

Ginsburg, H. P., & Opper, S. (1988). *Piaget's theory of intellectual development* (Third edition). Englewood Cliffs, NJ: Prentice Hall.

Hunt, D. E. (1971). *Matching models in education: the coordination of teaching methods with student characteristics.* Toronto: Ontario Institute for Studies in Education.

Jourard, S. M. (1968). *Disclosing man to himself.* Princeton, NJ: Van Nostrand.

Kitchener, K., & King, P. (1990). The reflective judgement model: Ten years of research. In *Adult development: Vol. 2. Models and methods in the study of adolescent and adult thought,* (pp. 63-78). New York: Praeger.

Kohlberg, L. (1969). Stage and sequence: The cognitive developmental approach to socialization. In D. Goslin (editor), *Handbook of socialization theory and research.* Chicago, IL: Rand McNally.

Kohlberg, L. (1979). *Meaning and measurement of moral development.* Worcester, MA: Clark University Press.

Kohlberg, L., & Mayer, R. (1972). Development as the aim of education. *Harvard Educational Review, 42*(4), 449-496.

Loevinger, J. (1976). *Ego development: Conceptions and theories.* San Francisco, CA: Jossey-Bass.

Maslow, A. (1970). *Motivation and personality* (Second edition). New York: Harper and Row.

Perry, W. G. (1970). *Forms of intellectual and ethical development in the college years.* New York: Holt, Rinehart and Winston.

Piaget, J. (1963). *Psychology of intelligence.* Paterson, NJ: Littlefield Adams.

Purkey, W. W., & Novak, J. M. (1984). *Inviting school success: A self-concept approach to teaching and learning* (Second edition). Belmont, CA: Wadsworth.

Sprinthall, N. A., & Sprinthall, R. C. (1990). *Educational Psychology: A Developmental Approach* (Fifth edition). New York: Mc Graw Hill.

Sprinthall, N. A., & Theis-Sprinthall, L. (1983). The teacher as adult learner: A cognitive-developmental view. In G. A. Griffin (editor), *Staff development,* (pp. 13-35). Chicago, IL: University of Chicago Press.

Sprinthall, N. A., & Theis-Sprinthall, L. (1987). Preservice teachers as adult learners; A new framework for teacher education. In M. Haberman & J. Backus (editors), *Advances in teacher education,* (pp. 35-56). Norwood, NJ: Ablex Publishers.

Theis-Sprinthall, L. (1984). Promoting the developmental growth of supervising teachers: Theory, research programs, and implications. *Journal of Teacher Education, 35,* 329-336.

Chapter 9
The Intentionally Inviting College

By Betty L. Siegel

Reaching for the world, as our lives do,
As all lives do, reaching that we may give
The best of what we are and hold as true:
Always it is by bridges that we live.
--Philip Larkin, "A Bridge for the Living"

As a co-founder of the International Alliance for Invitational Education, I have long been committed to adapting the principles of invitational education to the college setting. Just as the environment of a primary or secondary school can intentionally summons students to realize their potential in all areas of human endeavor and to see themselves as able, valuable, and self-directing (Purkey & Novak, 1984), a college campus also can and should become an environment in which faculty and students are encouraged to view education as a cooperative, collaborative activity where process is as important as product. Throughout my tenure as president of Kennesaw State College, I have therefore worked closely with my administrative team to use our people and places to create policies, processes, and programs specifically designed to invite, facilitate, and enhance educational achievement.

Through the decade of the 1980s and into the 1990s, the "crisis in higher education" has continued to be a harsh reality for today's colleges and universities. Dwindling resources, declining enrollments, debates over curriculum reform and academic freedom—these are just a few of the external and internal forces dramatically changing the face of higher education. And as Peter Smith (1991) points out, "the system's perceived inability to respond effectively [to these and other forces] is seriously eroding public confidence" (p. 26). Education bashing is not limited to our public schools; institutions of higher education are also under intense pressure to perform better.

Effectively dealing with political, societal, and economic forces requires a willingness on the part of educators to promote change and to look for new ways of coping. Faced with the prospect of "doing more with less," today's education leaders need a new perspective that will facilitate the tactics and strategies needed for institutional success. The invitational model (Purkey & Schmidt, 1987, p. 7) that emphasizes optimism, respect, trust, and intentionality can supply the fresh new perspective dictated by these harsh times. Though quite appropriate for more prosperous times, this approach is even more critical now. And at Kennesaw State College, we are in the process of making our institution an example of what can be accomplished when the college family is committed to the principles of invitationalism.

At a Crossroads

When I became president of the college in 1981, Kennesaw State was at a crossroads. Though we could have aspired to remain a typical, traditional senior college, our diverse student body made it imperative that we gradually change our mission and focus to meet their needs. Because we were a commuter college, more than two-thirds of our student body was employed full- or part-time. Our enrollment was at 4,000, and the average age of our students was 25.

Though we had a heavy emphasis on the liberal arts, the vast majority of our students pursued professional programs in business, education, and nursing. Community involvement and outreach was also not emphasized. Instead, we tended to have an "ivory tower" view of the world and were often referred to as a small "Harvard in the Pines." Student retention was becoming a critical problem. We were known as a way station—students stopped by for a year or two before transferring to other colleges and universities. Though Kennesaw had made the transition in 1978 from a junior college to a senior college, in many ways we were still thought of as a junior college.

We consequently had two choices. We could continue the posture that had served the college well in a less demanding time, or we could shift our focus, mission, service mode, and management style to create a more contemporary and inviting setting for contemporary students. We chose the latter strategy, turning to the invitational model as a means to re-examine our mission, to view our students in more positive ways, to think of administration as being facilitative and empowering, and to see the community as being an extension of our halls.

Fully committed to an invitational model, my first step as president was to invite our entire administrative team to share in this new vision of academic leadership. I turned to strong outside voices compatible with the invitational philosophy to help define this new approach. George Keller (1983), for example, in his extremely influential book, *Academic Strategy*, offers the following contrast between good education managers and traditional college administrators:

> Administrators prefer people, individual projects, specific routines; managers prefer ideas, linked initiatives, new ventures. Administrators tend to

be cool, amiably neutral, businesslike; managers tend to be spirited, committed, entrepreneurial. Administrators are usually cautious, passive, and conservative; managers are often risk-takers, active, and adventurous. Administrators love details and efficiency; managers love large objectives and effectiveness. Administrators are often clever and manipulative; managers are often gutsy and outspoken. Thus, the change to a greater future orientation and sharper management in education requires a willed shift of the psyche, a new courage to be, to do. (p. 68)

Committed to adopting this new management style, we never lost sight of the fact that "the invitational model requires unconditional respect for people" (Purkey & Schmidt, 1987, p. 12). As Keller (1983) further points out, "innovation does not require extra resources so much as it requires people to push innovation. Energetic professionals...are the primary ingredients of organizational vitality" (p. 64). United by the theme "Sharing the Vision, Shaping the Future," my administrative colleagues and I pursued a variety of strategies for building teamwork and for ensuring a powerful sense of ownership of all college policies and programs at all levels of the administrative hierarchy.

Dynamic Planning

To facilitate this newly-formed spirit of teamwork, we instituted a dynamic planning approach that emphasizes "strategic thinking" at all levels of the organization. Institutional planning became a shared responsibility and college-wide expectation. The planning process we adopted is guided by constant and continuous monitoring of institutional progress. Regular "team meetings" are held to monitor progress, maintain momentum, and promote change. Though all college administrations hold regular meetings, at Kennesaw State an invitational model is used at all levels to promote shared vision and common purpose, essential elements of sound strategic planning. Whether it be my meeting with the vice presidential staff, our deans meeting with department heads, or our entire administrative team meeting together in a retreat setting, the frame of reference is always how we can make the college more inviting. Our goal is not just to "get the job done" but to "get the right job done right by the right people." Our commitment to teamwork assumes that the college becomes a model institution only to the extent that its component parts—departments, programs, personnel, etc.—work together to face current and future challenges. It involves people acting decisively and in concert with the college's central strategy on invitational leadership.

In the early 1980s most colleges were hierarchical and depended on a "top-down" approach to management. Our management style was therefore considered very innovative. A positive affirmation of our innovative emphasis on building teamwork came in 1985, when Kennesaw State was named in a national study conducted by George Mason University as one of the nation's top twenty colleges "on the move" (Gilley, Fulmer, & Reithlingshoefer, 1986). The results of this study, published in book form under the title *Searching for Academic Excellence*, affirmed that "teamwork...is a crucial aspect of life at [all twenty selected] institutions and represents a genuine divergence from standard functioning at the majority of higher education institutions. Putting together an effective top administrative team was one of the first priorities of these presidents when they assumed their current posts" (Gilley *et al.*, 1986, p. 12).

"View of the Future" Project

To foster a similar spirit of teamwork throughout the faculty and staff, we initiated during the first year of my presidency a "View of the Future" project in order to clarify a new shared vision of how we wanted the college to develop. As Warren Bennis (1989) points out, one of the marks of a successful leader is the ability to enroll others in his or her vision (pp. 155-172). We therefore invited the entire faculty and staff to participate in this project, asking them for their recommendations in four key areas: What should be our mission? How can we personalize the teaching/learning process to enhance and invite student success? What are the publics that we serve? What can administrators do to be more supportive of teachers, staff, and students?

This intensive, year-long study of our college allowed us to focus on our people, programs, policies, processes, and place. Most notably, the study encouraged us to carefully examine what we were and were not doing for our students. We identified behaviors and policies that were "unintentionally disinviting" to our students, focusing on those elements of the Kennesaw State experience that made them feel unwelcome and uncomfortable. These ranged from small issues, such as inadequate campus signs, to more significant concerns about poor advisement procedures. We subsequently came to realize that a large number of our students, especially nontraditional students who attended classes in the evening, felt disassociated from mainstream college life. We also recognized that our rapidly-growing student body put us in danger of becoming impersonal, and that we were beginning to lose the intimacy and the warmth we cherished as a small college.

Though we had programs already in place to facilitate the success of our students, our research revealed that these resources remained largely untapped or were short sighted. In fact, many students admitted that they were unaware that these services were available to them. We also had a relatively low retention rate, suggesting that many of our students did not develop a strong commitment to the college. College life was at a minimum. We were a "PCP college"—our students moved from the parking lot to the classroom and back to the parking lot.

"Freshman Experience Seminar"

Having considered a variety of ways to act on the findings of the "View of the Future" study, we chose to initiate a "Freshman Experience Seminar" that would enhance our students' social and academic integration into the college while providing a forum within which we could urge them to become the architects of their own success. Ernest Boyer's (1987) highly informative study, *College: The Undergraduate Experience in America*, concludes that a caring college will make the freshman year a top priority, ensuring that all campus personnel are sensitive to the special needs of incoming students (pp. 43-57).

Based on John Gardner's "University 101" class at the University of South Carolina (Gardner, 1989), our KSC 101 freshman experience program is designed to introduce freshmen and transfer students to the college and its resources. This class provides students with opportunities for the development of the personal competencies necessary for success in college and in life. Not only does it establish links between individual needs and the resources available within the college community, but the program also places a great deal of emphasis on increasing self- and others-awareness. At some point in the course of each KSC 101 class, students are required to work together in teams and are urged to respect and value the differences they find in their classmates. More importantly, students are encouraged to see themselves as able, valuable, and responsible.

As important as it is for students, the freshman seminar may be even more important and valuable to the faculty who teach it, for it provides an unparalleled opportunity to reach students by developing high-quality mentoring relationships with them. The faculty members who participate in the workshops and training sessions specially designed to prepare them to teach this course are made more aware of the need to send positive invitations to their

students. They are also encouraged to pursue the personal meaning and caring nature of teaching.

Gordon Klopf and Joan Harrison (1982) assert that faculty
members who care enough to invest in their students are like
midwives who help students find a new identity (p. 6). And this
course makes the faculty much more sensitive to the difficult
transition first-year students face as they try to prove themselves
as capable college students. All key administrators (including the
president, vice presidents, deans, and department heads), along
with most of our faculty, have attended the training sessions for
this program. Though all of us have not had the opportunity to
teach a section of the course, our awareness of the process and the
value of the experience has proven extremely valuable in our
efforts to be an inviting college.

KSC 101 is perhaps the hallmark program that marks Kennesaw
State as an "invitational" college. Systematic evaluations of this
program make it clear that it has had a direct positive effect on
retention, and both students and faculty praise the opportunities
it creates for developing mentoring relationships. Not only does
the program benefit our weaker "developmental" students, but
our research clearly indicates that it also greatly enhances the
success potential of our better students. This rigorous course
carries five hours credit, and students are often surprised at the
amount of work required for what some thought would be an
"easy" class. Though the course is currently part of our Department of Liberal Studies, we have worked hard to develop a
department-like structure for the entire KSC 101 program, giving
the faculty who teach it the opportunity to hold regular meetings
to refine and strengthen the course content and to share ideas and
experiences.

Faculty Growth

Another positive outcome of the course was the powerful

lesson it supplied about the value and necessity of providing our faculty with a variety of professional-development opportunities. We have consequently implemented programs designed to invite our faculty to grow professionally. It is not enough just to hire outstanding teachers. Like all professionals, faculty members expect appropriate recognition for their past and current achievements, and they require appropriate renewal opportunities to ensure their continued excellence. At one time or another, virtually all teachers experience some degree of faculty burnout, unrest, or dissatisfaction, making it necessary for them to refresh their spirits and to renew their commitment to the teaching profession.

The ability to renew one's spirit obviously plays a key role in any profession. The seventh and most important habit that Stephen Covey (1987) explores in *The Seven Habits of Highly Effective People* is renewal. He uses the following story to illustrate his point (p. 287). Suppose you come upon someone in the woods working feverishly to saw down a tree. The person looks exhausted and explains that he has been sawing on the tree for over five hours. You suggest that it might be helpful to take a break and sharpen the saw. The person responds emphatically, "I don't have time to sharpen the saw because I'm too busy sawing." The point of the story is obvious. One of the keys to inviting others to succeed is the ability to invite the self to succeed. Occasionally, everyone in the college community, especially the teaching faculty, needs to pause and sharpen the saw of academic excellence.

The Center for Excellence in Teaching and Learning (CETL) serves as Kennesaw State's most important agency of faculty development and renewal. CETL provides professional growth opportunities through seminars, workshops, newsletters, faculty grants, and summer research stipends. These programs allow our faculty to be professionally inviting to themselves as they consider innovative approaches for expanding their repertoire of teaching strategies, especially those that affirm the great diversity of our student body. CETL's quarterly publication, *Reaching through*

Teaching, featuring articles by Kennesaw State College faculty members on innovative approaches to enhancing the classroom experience, has received numerous awards from the Council for the Advancement and Support of Education (CASE).

Leadership Program

CETL also administers our highly successful and innovative Leadership Kennesaw State College program. This initiative provides an opportunity for our teaching faculty to assume leadership roles throughout both the campus committee structure and the local community. The objective of this innovative program is to invite, cultivate, encourage, and nurture faculty leadership development, following the model that chambers of commerce have used in recent years to promote community leadership. This year-long study program is designed especially for a select group of involved, dynamic, and promising faculty members and department heads who have expressed a desire to prepare themselves to meet the leadership challenges of higher education in the future.

The program participants are better prepared to understand the "big picture" internally and externally and to take responsibility for shared leadership in moving the college forward in the future. Emphasizing team building, interpersonal relationships, commitment to community, and a host of other invitational frames of reference, a series of eight focus sessions are held during the academic year—beginning and ending with a two-day retreat. Previous sessions have focused on such topics as a study of ethics in higher education, the formation of discipline-specific conferences on improving teaching, and a series of seminars on key issues such as teaching critical thinking and defining academic freedom.

Similar leadership programs are also conducted for the staff and for the students. Both Student Leadership Kennesaw State and Staff Leadership Kennesaw State have been highly effective initiatives. In fact, all three of these innovative leadership programs have received national recognition and have been studied as potential models for other institutions. Certainly part of their success can be attributed to the fact that they are based on the four principles of the invitational model: optimism, respect, trust, and intentionality. These four elements supply the participants with a consistent stance that fosters inviting actions in all of their activities, both on the campus and off.

Honoring Diversity

One of the common denominators connecting all of these special programs designed to invite student and faculty success and development is an urgent need to honor the great diversity found throughout the college. Diversity has become a focal point, not just at Kennesaw State, but throughout the country. In fact, of the many societal changes affecting higher education, none is more prominent than the extraordinary diversity found at our colleges and universities. Not only are our campuses hosts to traditional students who enter college at eighteen and graduate four years later, but recent studies show that almost 50 percent of the nation's college students are twenty-four years of age or older (*Fall Enrollment Report*, 1990). Because they work full- or part-time jobs and have family obligations, many of these students also take longer than four years to complete their degrees. According to the latest figures available from the University System of Georgia, less than 35 percent of the first-time, full- time freshman who enrolled in 1984 in one of the System's 34 colleges or universities graduated within five years.

When combined with the growing number of minorities and international students enrolling in college, these nontraditional students bring a great diversity to our college campuses. In fact, at numerous institutions, including Kennesaw State, nontraditional students are becoming the new majority. And this diverse body of students deserves an educational environment committed to accommodating the specific needs of each individual group. They need to be intentionally invited to see themselves as able, valuable, and responsible. They need to know that their differences are respected, and that they can expect a pattern of behavior that sends signals of optimism, trust, and respect.

Patricia Cross, former chair of the American Association for Higher Education Board of Directors, is a noted spokesperson on a number of educational issues, and she often uses the analogy that today's colleges must build new access ramps to the super highways that form postsecondary education. In the past, when there was little diversity, most traffic on these highways traveled at the same rate of speed and in the same direction. Now, however, there are many different types of vehicles and drivers—company vans, foreign models, and even classy antiques. Cross likens our role as teachers as being similar to traffic cops who are asked to meet twenty assorted vehicles going at different speeds and escort them in a convoy through the maze of academic requirements for a particular course or program of study.

A major force in our campus-wide commitment to honor diversity is a strong push to enhance minority participation in all aspects of our college life. Operating on the belief that access and excellence are not polar opposites, we have planned and implemented several programs designed to invite the success of our diverse student body. These intentionally inviting programs encourage faculty to use different strategies in dealing with diversity and encourage students to avail themselves of the opportunity to enroll in the total college experience. We strive to honor diversity at all levels of the campus experience, creating a supportive climate for our African-American students and our other minority populations. Our goal is the formation of a support network which connects all students to caring faculty, administrators, and peers.

Faculty Recruitment and Retention

Throughout the late 1970s and early 1980s, Kennesaw State employed only six black faculty members, less than five percent of our total teaching staff. Because most of these individuals lacked the doctorate and were hired as instructors, turnover was high and morale was low. It is no wonder that only two percent of the student body in the fall of 1982 was black. When I became president of the college, I was deeply troubled by this situation. As a proud public institution with a commitment to diversity, it was essential for us to give a high priority and a strong commitment to the recruitment and retention of black faculty, staff, and students.

In 1990, 25 of the 266 full-time teaching faculty were black, giving Kennesaw State one of the highest (if not the highest) percentages of black faculty among similar senior colleges in the University System of Georgia. Black faculty have been successfully recruited and retained in all four of the college's schools and in most instructional departments. Seventy percent of our black colleagues possess a terminal degree, and four out of ten hold the rank of full or associate professor. The contributions and morale of our black colleagues have never been higher. In addition, the number of black students enrolled tripled from 1982 to 1989. Our black enrollment in the fall of 1988 reflected a 19 percent increase over the fall of 1987, and a 71 percent increase over the last five years.

My administrative team firmly believes that real progress in black faculty and student recruitment and retention on a predominantly white campus cannot be achieved unless the institutional climate for blacks is receptive, inviting, and supportive. As the invitational model dictates, we strive to guard against sending unintentionally disinviting messages to any members of the college family. And more importantly, we strive to send intentional invitations that people are able, valuable, and responsible. Pursuant to that goal, we have moved over the years from a celebration of Black History Week to a celebration of Black History Month, and we are working toward an ultimate goal of establishing a year-long, curriculum-wide focus that ensures a greater understanding of all aspects of this country's cultural diversity, including our proud heritage of black history.

We at Kennesaw State are committed to inclusion, not exclusion, refusing to accept the myth that access and excellence are mutually exclusive. We also maintain a strong commitment to honor the diverse appeals for affirmation that come to us from on and off the campus, to provide opportunities for personal and professional growth for all of our faculty and staff members, and to foster initiatives that will allow us to facilitate increased participation of black faculty, staff, and students in all aspects of the college mission and function.

Intentionally Inviting the Community

Along with our efforts to establish an administrative team committed to the invitational model, to create positive success experiences for our students, faculty, and staff, and to honor diversity all levels of the campus, we are also fully committed to making the college intentionally inviting to the various communities we serve. For example, we are strong proponents of the national movement to transform institutions of higher education into "interactive" universities and colleges. Alan Ostar (cited in Gilley, 1990), former President of the American Association of State Colleges and Universities, offers the following definition of an interactive institution:

> [An institution] whose basic developmental strategy is to form an active and reciprocal partnership with the leadership (business, civic, and political) of its community or region, a partnership focused on the common goal of shaping a community that

> is strong and equitable, both economically and socially. Predominantly "others centered" in orientation, the interactive [institution] is willing and able to involve its community citizens as "stakeholders" or co-owners in the [institution's] future. This orientation contrasts with the more classic [college or] university, an institution partly characterized as aloof and separate from society, serving as a detached critic rather than an active participant. (pp. 9-10)

At Kennesaw State, we have already begun our transformation into an "interactive" regional college. Having rejected the "ivory tower" fortress mind-set common among some institutions of higher education, we made a conscious effort to reach out to the community and to invite the public onto our campus. Nowhere is our attempt to meet the needs of the community more evident than in our program development. Having carefully examined community needs, we added graduate programs in business administration and in education, and we are currently developing a Master of Public Administration degree. Many teachers also choose Kennesaw State College to fulfill their requirements for post-baccalaureate certification. In 1989, we also established the nation's first undergraduate degree program in professional sales.

In addition, our A. L. Burruss Institute of Public Service links faculty expertise with community needs by holding public forums and seminars for public officials, local citizens, faculty, and students. The college has also won national awards for our Small Business Development Center, which provides specialized programs and training to family businesses. These are just a few of the many programs we have developed to meet the needs of our service region. Though all colleges and universities strive to refine existing programs and to develop new ones, we make sure that we invite and carefully consider community input before we initiate any new courses of study or community services. Given this invitational philosophy, it is little wonder that during the past ten years our enrollment has risen dramatically from 4,000 to 11,000 students, making Kennesaw State Georgia's largest senior college, characterized in 1991 by the *U. S. News and World Report* as one of the South's two "rising stars" in higher education.

Our commitment to interact with all sectors of the community, creating a powerful group of "stakeholders" who share our mission of excellence, includes a willingness to listen to and learn from our region's business, political, and community leaders. Now more than ever, the nation's colleges and universities need the support of the private sector. Not only do they supply much needed financial support, but they can also be invited to share ideas, advice, and direction.

John Clendenin (1989), Chairman and Chief Executive Officer of BellSouth Corporation, speaks often about the need for connections between institutes of higher education and the business community. He argues that if the strengths and talents of the leaders from the education community, from the political community, and from the business community are intertwined together, they will create "a formidable braid of three threads" which when woven together through cooperation forms a unit "much stronger than any single strand could ever be." He concludes that these three strands are essential for "reweaving this country's unraveling educational tapestry." In order to ensure that the college family has many opportunities to hear a variety of local leaders, we instituted our Enterprise 2000 Lecture Series. This initiative has brought many of our region's most prominent business leaders to our campus for a series of lectures and workshops.

Along with our commitment to forge strong ties with the local business leaders, we have also formed a unique consortium uniting our region's public colleges, technical institutes, and school systems. The mission of this education consortium is to work together to foster an exemplary "education culture" in which the community values education highly, appreciates education's role in economic development and the quality of life not only in the community but the entire region, takes pride in the quality of public educational services available, and aggressively supports the advancement of education for all ages. This seamless web of educational opportunities will allow area educators to work together as partners to foster a superior quality of life by ensuring that there is no break in the lifelong learning potential offered to the citizens of our region.

Importance of Place

Along with the intentionally inviting initiatives put in place through our people, policies, processes, and programs, we have also been attentive to the importance of place. Boyer (1989) suggests that the look and feel of a campus can greatly influence prospective students:

> When we asked students what influenced them most during their visit to a campus, about half mentioned "the friendliness of students we met." But it was the buildings, the trees, the walkways, the well-kept lawns—that overwhelmingly won out. The appearance of the campus is, by far, the most influential characteristic during campus visits, and we gained the distinct impression that when it comes to recruiting students, the director of buildings and grounds may be more important than the academic dean. (p. 17)

Though how an institution looks might affect a student's decision to attend, the institutional climate of the college will certainly have a greater effect on his or her decision to remain. A caring and inviting college must therefore be very attentive to maintaining a campus-wide congenial atmosphere that is always conducive to learning.

A careful consideration of the importance of place has long

been a key ingredient of Kennesaw State's institutional effectiveness. Most commuter colleges are not necessarily recognized for their beautiful campuses, but rather for the efficiency with which they manage large groups of drive-in students. At Kennesaw State, however, we have put forth an extraordinary effort to create a positive ambiance for our students, faculty, staff, and many community visitors. Our 152-acre campus reveals a balance between the demands of a growing student body and a concern for preserving the natural environment. Tree-lined walkways and rolling hills provide a serene environment which invites our commuter students to stay on the campus, while a new business building and performing arts theater offer increased classroom space and comfort.

A Fluid Process

Perhaps the biggest asset of the invitational model in college management is the fluid nature of the process. It allows administrators to be flexible and to be able to change, based on the resources available and the needs of a service region. It encourages all college personnel to reanalyze and to refocus and to accept that the final work never gets finished. The inviting administrator, teacher, and staff member must remain attentive to the challenges of never-ending change. When Kennesaw State's faculty asked for a stronger voice in our governance procedure, we created a special faculty caucus to meet separately and as part of our College Senate.

When a recent budget crisis forced the state of Georgia to deny pay raises for non-teaching faculty, administrators, and staff personnel, we held a day-long retreat in which elected representatives from these groups met to discuss salary issues and to identify other staff concerns. One of the outcomes of this retreat was the formation of a staff caucus similar to our faculty caucus. Not only have we invited the faculty and staff to communicate their concerns, but we are also very attentive to such crucial issues as curriculum reform. During the coming decade, for example, we will closely examine the important role student volunteerism will play in our core curriculum.

The "Senior Seminar"

This emphasis on refinement and innovation encourages us to seek new ways of inviting success. Greatly impressed by the overwhelmingly positive response to our freshman experience program, we are now developing a similar "senior seminar" course designed to bridge the gap between a student's senior year and his or her professional career. The class is organized around the same model of invitationalism that can be utilized in virtually any work setting. Roughly half of the course introduces the students to the value of this theory of functioning. A series of readings, lectures, and exercises focuses on the four principal components of the invitational model: being personally inviting with self, being personally inviting with others, being professionally inviting with self, and being professionally inviting with others.

Because the class is designed especially for seniors, the students enrolled have already proven their ability to perform on an individual level. They have passed a number of courses in the core curriculum and in their chosen major as well as a few elective courses. All of these accomplishments label them as proficient individual performers. Their success in the work place, however, will depend not just on individual performance, but also on the relationships they develop with their co-workers and employers. The passage from their senior year to their professional career will force them to move from being individual performers in a familiar setting to being team players in an unfamiliar setting. They will be encouraged to assume leadership roles and to take responsibility for the success of others.

The controlling theme of the class is "we make our lives by understanding them, and we enjoy success by balancing the different relationships and responsibilities that make up our lives." The remainder of the course, consequently, emphasizes relationships of all kinds—not just with workmates, but also with family, friends, and the entire community. Traditional college courses increase competence in a particular skill or discipline, but they rarely address the challenges of daily life, such as learning to balance professional goals with personal needs. I therefore use a variety of sources—fiction, poetry, movies, essays, guest lecturers, etc.—to generate discussions about human relationships.

A common denominator running throughout the course is that increasing their self-confidence by expanding their self-knowledge will better prepare the students to meet the new challenges that lie ahead. After all, a greater knowledge of self will give them better control of the transition they are facing. And, of course, self-knowledge is inextricably bound to being personally and professionally inviting with self, and forming positive relationships is inextricably bound to being personally and professionally inviting with others. As a long marcher in the ranks of invitational educators, I find this class a microcosm of the principles of invitational education.

It Is by Invitations that We Educate

Philip Larkin (1989) concludes one of my favorite poems with the following stanza:

> Reaching for the world, as our lives do,
> As all lives do, reaching that we may give
> The best of what we are and hold as true:
> Always it is by bridges that we live. (p. 204)

We at Kennesaw State pride ourselves on being the kind of master bridge builders that Larkin so eloquently describes. We have formed powerful connections to span the gulfs that often separate college administrators from one another and from the teaching faculty. We have encouraged the faculty to form strong mentoring relationships with our students. We believe that an inviting teacher is a master teacher and that a master teacher is a master bridge builder. We have also worked hard to bridge the troubled waters that often keep the ivory towers of higher education isolated from the surrounding community. We have lowered the drawbridge that opened our classrooms to a host of nontraditional students. The principles of invitational education have supplied the concrete, steel, arches, and cables of all of these powerful "bridges." As Larkin points out, "always it is by bridges that we live." And always it is by invitations that we educate.

References

Bennis, Warren. (1989). *On becoming a leader.* New York: Addison-Wesley.

Boyer, Ernest. (1987). *College: The undergraduate experience in America.* New York: Harper & Row.

Clendenin, John. (1989). Reweaving the country's unraveling educational tapestry. Keynote address at the Chancellor's Forum, East Carolina University, January 3.

Covey, Stephen. (1989). *The seven habits of highly effective people.* New York: Simon & Schuster.

Gardner, John. (1989). Starting a freshman seminar program. In Upcraft, M. Lee, & Gardner, John (editors), *The freshman year experience,* pp. 238-249. San Francisco, CA: Jossey Bass.

Gilley, J. Wade. (1990). *The interactive university: A source of American revitalization.* Washington, DC: American Association of State Colleges and Universities.

Gilley, J. Wade, Fulmer, Kenneth A., & Reithlingshoefer, Sally J. (editors). (1986). *Searching for academic excellence: Twenty colleges and universities on the move and their leaders.* New York: Macmillan.

Keller, George. (1983). *Academic strategy: The management revolution in American higher education.* Baltimore, MD: The Johns Hopkins University Press.

Klopf, Gordon J., & Harrison, Joan S. (1982). *Mentoring, paper 5.* New York: Center for Leadership Development, Bank Street College.

Larkin, Philip. (1989). Bridge for the living. In Thwaite, Anthony (editor),

Philip Larkin: Collected poems, pp. 203-204. New York: Farrar Straus Giroux.

Purkey, William Watson, & Novak, John M. (1984) *Inviting school success: A self-concept approach to teaching and learning.* Belmont, CA: Wadsworth.

Purkey, William Watson, & Schmidt, John J. (1987). *The inviting relationship: An expanded perspective for professional counseling.* Englewood Cliffs, NJ: Prentice-Hall.

Smith, Peter. (1991). Beyond budgets: Changing for the better. *Educational Record,* 72(2), 26-28.

U. S. Department of Education. (1990). *Fall enrollment report.* Washington, DC: U. S. Government Printing Office.

Inviting
Others and Yourself

Chapter 10

Invitational Theory and Counselling

By William B. Stafford

We are constantly invited to be who we are.
--*Henry David Thoreau*

Introduction

Let me tell you a story. It is not my story, but it is a good story. It is a story told by a physician (Engel, 1987), and it took place in 1938. It is a story about a young man named Sidney.

Sidney was in his early twenties in 1938, during the Great Depression years. Prior to this time, Sidney had been a typical young man, energetic, curious, and full of life. Recently, however, Sidney had changed, and he was the antithesis of what others had perceived him to be. He stopped looking for a job, he became listless, and he took to his room a great deal of the time. His mother was concerned for his well-being, and she was convinced his morose attitude was a direct product of the depression years. All he needed, she reckoned, was a job to lift his spirits and get him started again, so she prevailed upon her brother-in-law, who owned a delicatessen, to give Sidney a job. The brother-in-law was not thrilled with this idea, as he did not need another worker, and he was concerned because he was not able to pay Sidney a salary. Sidney's mother prevailed, and her brother-in-law finally agreed to give Sidney a minor job for which Sidney could have an occasional snack from the delicatessen. This was fine with Sidney's mother, as she was convinced that productive and useful work was all that Sidney needed.

In a very short period of time, it appeared that Sidney's mother had been correct, for Sidney's whole demeanor changed and the "old Sidney" seemed to be back. He was full of life and interest again, and his mother felt justified in her diagnosis that he needed work to lift himself from the doldrums.

However, this was to be short-lived, for one day Sidney came home and sadly announced that he had been fired. When his mother called her brother-in-law to protest, she found her protests were in vain for her brother-in-law would not have Sidney back because of his "disgusting habits."

"What disgusting habits?" demanded Sidney's mother. It evolved that the customers in the delicatessen were upset that Sidney was often dipping his hand in the pickle barrel, and licking the brine from his fingers. Shortly after his dismissal, Sidney retreated to his prior ways of listlessness and cutting himself off from the world. His mother was again convinced that all of this had happened because of the humiliation of losing his job.

Not long after his dismissal, however, Sidney collapsed and was taken to the hospital where Dr. Engel was a young intern. Engel recognized the classic symptoms of Addison's disease, which Sidney had probably been maintaining by indulging in the salt of the pickle brine. Sidney's mother, however, insisted it was all a result of the depression. Engel stated:

> Standing together at the foot of the same bed and
> looking at the same young person, I saw Addison's
> disease and she saw a depressed, discouraged

> son, bedeviled also perhaps by an "upset stom-
> ach" to boot, the consequence of sipping pickle
> brine, no doubt. Contrasting views as to what we
> were looking at yielded different views of what
> was there. In other words, it is not just "where you
> stand determines what you **think** you see," but
> "where you **think** you stand determines what you
> **think** you see."....My confident pronouncement
> that Sidney's condition could be fully explained
> by adrenal insufficiency surely must have evoked
> in his mother a response...."it's what-this-terrible-
> Depression-is-doing-to-our-young-people." For
> obviously, if I was [sic] right, she must be wrong.
> (Engel, 1987, pp. 23-24.)

Engel's story does not stop here, for he used Sidney's story to examine the notion of the objective reality of the detached scientist which Engel saw as the "legacy of seventeenth-century mechanism, reductionism, and mind-body dualism of Newton and Descartes", i.e., the "scientific" view of medicine which is often stated, "where you stand determines what you see" (Engel, 1987, p. 24).

Modern medicine and counseling psychology, the latter which often seems to wish to imitate the precision of the medical model dating back perhaps to the work and influence of John B. Watson, often tend to ignore the "uncertainty principle" of quantum physics. Most simply stated, the uncertainty principle reminds us that every act of measurement, as well as the mental processing of the so-called objective viewer, introduces uncertainties into that observation.

> In a word, quantum physics led physicists to
> rediscover the mind, the "where you think you
> stand" that determines the "what you think you
> see."...So too are the mental operations and pro-
> cesses whereby we ascribe the separateness and

boundaries to what are in fact to one degree or
another actually dynamic continua of transac-
tions, wholes...Sidney's "depression," so central
to his mother's "view," was something quite apart
from the adrenal failure I so clearly saw. If depression existed at all, it surely could be explained by
his adrenal disease....Almost fifty years have
passed since, in my mind, I dismissed Sidney's
mother's formulation. Now I know she was right,
to a degree; and so was I, but also only to a degree.
Today, I would wonder to what extent Sidney's
frame of mind may have contributed to setting the
stage for an autoimmune process that ultimately
culminated in adrenal atrophy and the Addisonian
crises, just as I would wonder to what extent my
ability to intervene with effective hormone re-
placement may have served to bring to an end a
vicious cycle of economic depression → psychological depression → autoimmune response →
adrenal insufficiency → psychological depression.
I would even wonder what influence my fascina-
tion with Sidney's story may have had on his
subsequent course. He did well. (Engel, 1987, p.
24).

Engel's story is helpful to us in viewing human interactions. His
story provides us with a perspective which is crucial in understanding invitational theory, as invitational theory is built on
concepts of perceptual psychology which are closely aligned with
Engel's "where you **think** you stand determines what you **think**
you see." In a very real sense, Engel's story set the stage for
invitational theory and its relationship to counseling.

Counseling and Perceptions of Trust

Erikson (1963) stated the basic developmental task and the basic structure of identity lies in the issues of trust versus mistrust. Hamachek (1985) has added to our perspective of this notion of trust. In his examination of trust in Eriksonian terms, Hamachek observed that trust is not an either/or proposition, but rather the healthy, functioning individual, who while having a basic sense of trust in others and his or her world, typically has at least a modicum of skepticism and mistrust. That is, the more balanced individual has a basic sense of trust in the way the individual perceives the world, but the person is not pollyannaish in his or her view of the world, since the person's outlook is also tempered by life experiences. Those life experiences urge the person to move with some caution and to "read" any given situation carefully before making a commitment to a set of circumstances. More commonly, this is called good sense or prudence, or, as Engel stated, "where you **think** you stand determines what you **think** you see."

Trust remains the cornerstone of development and the structure of one's personality. While what the person often presents suggests a stability and evenness of the individual's personality structure, our experiences tell us this is not always the case, and this basic notion of personality may be deceptive. When a person is in a stressful situation where the individual's trust has been violated, that stability and evenness may appear illusory. Consider, for example, the individual who feels betrayed by another who is significant, and who previously had the individual's unqualified trust (e.g., a spouse). When such trust has been violated, the whole personality structure of the betrayed individual appears to be altered. Where, before, the person seemed solid and unshakable, a basic violation of trust can literally transform the person's whole mien. Moustakas (1972) addressed this issue effectively when he stated:

The confrontation shakes up the individual, puts
[the person] in a turbulent state, and forces [the
person] to use new energies and resources to come
to terms with [his or her] life--to find a new way to
self....In loneliness, some compelling, essential
aspect of life is suddenly challenged, threatened,
altered, denied. At such times only by entering
into loneliness, by steeping oneself in the experience and allowing it to take its course and to reveal
itself is there hope that one's world will achieve
harmony and unity. Then the person can begin
again, born as a new self, with openness, sponta-
neity, and trust. (p. 21)

Trust, when typically viewed as a paradigm, often resembles a
pyramid, with trust at the broad base upon which all else rests. In
most circumstances, this is quite probably an adequate representation. However, this representation, as suggested above, may be
deceptive, particularly when a person is in a very stressful situation
where trust has been betrayed. As we look at the altered representation of the violated personality, an **inverted** pyramid, with trust
shifted to the apex, seems much more representative of the personality structure. The personality now lacks the broad, solid base, and
teeters precariously instead on the inverted apex which lacks
stability.

So it is with counseling. Typically, clients come to the counselor
shaken by one or more situations which have destabilized their
center to the point they are top heavy, uncertain, their whole
perceptual field in disarray, and perhaps above all, doubting
themselves and others. In this unsteady and quite often unfamiliar
setting, the client comes seeking a reliable and trustworthy person
against whom to cast his or her uncertainties in an attempt to regain
a sense of being centered with one's self and one's world.

What a precarious beginning for the counselor! A very anxious
client recently told a counselor after several meetings:

> You were on trial in those first sessions. I needed
> so desperately to be able to trust you, yet I was
> filled with nothing but distrust because of all that
> had happened to me. I didn't trust myself nor
> anybody else, and yet I knew that if I could not
> connect with someone enough to share the hor-
> rors within me, I would most certainly go under.
> I read you as carefully as another could possibly
> read a person, particularly under all the stress and
> anxiety I was experiencing, and it was finally a do-
> or-die situation. I trusted you with my most
> guarded and most frightening secrets, and I
> watched your every reaction. Had you flinched, I
> would have been out of there like a shot and you
> would never have seen me again. BUT, you didn't!
> You accepted me in all my craziness, and you
> invited me to join with you in finding and fighting
> my demons. You trusted yourself and you trusted
> me to join in this search, and I knew it would be all
> right. (Stafford, 1991)

What an awesome task having that kind of trust from another, for it invokes a strong sense of responsibility. Yet, without a sense of shared trust and the subsequent shared responsibility, it is unlikely that anything of significance will occur in the counseling relationship.

Moustakas (1972) expressed this relationship vividly when he stated:

> This spirit of life, this trust in one being connected
> with other beings, this innocence that feels deeply
> that my tears are your sorrows, that my joy is your
> laughter, is strikingly present in infants and very
> young children as they first encounter life. In their
> innocence and trust, self-communication and self-
> expression flow outwardly to touch and awaken,

to keep the faith that being alive in spirit, feeling,
and creation is the essential commitment of being
human. (Moustakas, 1972, p. 7.)

The Relationship of Invitational Theory
to Counseling

Purkey suggested a way of looking at the relationship of
invitational theory to counseling in his discussion of the notions of
"context" and "content" (W. W. Purkey, personal communication,
October 7, 1991). Context, in a perceptual sense, provides the
ground of the experience, while content represents the **figure** of the
experience. Relating this directly to invitational theory and counseling, invitational theory represents the ground (context) in which
to understand the figure (content) of the process of counseling.
Invitational theory is broad and pervasive in examining the myriad
of human interactions, and takes on yet a different form when
counseling is examined within this context.

Counseling is viewed by those embracing the invitational
stance as being among the most personal and intense of human
interactions. It is an experience into which neither client nor
counselor should enter lightly. Both counselor and client share
risks in coming together, and both must adopt assumptions about
the other in the process. Since the counselor is considered the
professional and the helper in this relationship, it is the counselor's
responsibility to convey to the client his or her willingness to
engage with the client in this endeavor, and to make a covenant to
this relationship with the client both professionally and personally.
In the invitational model, the counselor must have a reasonably
clear sense of the client's view of his or her world, so that the
counselor can convey in a way understood and accepted by the
client that the counselor not only has this sense of the client's world,
but also the counselor perceives the client as being valuable,
capable, and responsible. In addition, the counselor must also

convey that he or she is one who can be trusted both in terms of skills and commitment to the client. In an invitational sense, it is the counselor who must extend the invitation to the client to enter into the counseling relationship, even though it may have been the client who initiated the original contact with the counselor. Additionally, it is the counselor's responsibility to understand where the counselor **thinks** he or she stands, which will be a part of the broader perception of what the counselor **thinks** he or she sees in the client.

In the very initial contact of a counseling relationship, everything seems to rest upon the client's perception of the counselor as a person and as a professional in terms of the counselor's trustworthiness and ability to understand. Wrenn (1990) stated that in most human interactions, we are valued by our clients and our colleagues for our personal attributes, and that our professional attributes are assessed by those personal qualities. Wrenn's point is clear that we cannot separate the professional from the personal as they are closely intertwined. But, how does the counselor convey to the client that the counselor is trustworthy and capable of the task?

Invitational theory provides a stance for the development of a counseling relationship. The counselor must intentionally invite the client into the counseling relationship. Two crucial issues become fused immediately in the encounter between client and counselor: **inviting** and **intentionality**.

Inviting

Given that we share some common understanding of the act of inviting, it is equally as important to understand the **process** by which we would be inviting. Purkey has provided us with an anatomy of an invitation, that is, what perceptions and dynamics are involved in the inviting act, or where we **think** we stand determines what we **think** we see. In examining Purkey's anatomy of an invitation, we need to remind ourselves of the basic issues of perceptual psychology involved. These would include minimally such concepts as figure and ground; perceptual field and personal understandings; perceived reality and objective reality; and issues of trust affecting one's sense of self and others. When Purkey presented his anatomy of an invitation, he did so to cover the broad range of human interactions. In discussing counseling issues, however, some of these concepts appear to be too specific and prescriptive, and more related to teaching perhaps than to counseling. For example, when Purkey discussed specific "techniques" and "approaches," they appear to go beyond the parameters of counseling within a perceptual framework, which needs to be more fluid and spontaneous in order to be sensitive and responsive to the individual client. This more fluid and spontaneous nature of the interaction also relates to the skills and personhood of the counselor, who must remain vigilant not to violate the client's sense of capability, responsibility, or worth in this unique relationship. A modification of Purkey's anatomy of an invitation is presented in Figure 1 in an attempt to respond to some of these concerns.

Figure 1 presents two different sets of perceptions, i.e., the perceptions of the counselor/inviter and the perceptions of the client/invited. Additionally, these perceptions are further subdivided in terms of how both the inviter and the invited perceive their worlds in general (i.e., where they think they stand and what they think they see), and how each might perceive the process of inviting from these different perspectives. The broader understanding of the process for both the inviter and the invited is necessary to have a greater sense of the dynamics involved in both extending/not extending and accepting/not accepting the invitation to the possibilities of counseling.

Perhaps one of the most basic questions to be raised is, "what is this an invitation to, and what is it going to cost me?"--A question which has implications for both counselor and client. For the counselor, it involves a myriad of considerations, including a determination of what the client entering the counselor's perceptual world seems to want and need, but is often unable to ask. The counselor must also consider the role he or she can play should the invitation be accepted by the client.

Most simply put, the process being presented here, in an invitational sense, is setting the stage for the counselor to communicate to the client that this is a safe place where the client may examine issues and where the client has the possibility to experience growth. Additionally, the counselor must convey, at least minimally, that he or she possesses basic skills of helping at both a personal and a professional level. Finally, the counselor must convey his or her dependability to the client, i.e., "You can rely upon me to walk through whatever issues are important to you, and they will not drive me away." All of these issues are summed up in Engel's statement of where the counselor **thinks** he or she stands determines what the counselor **thinks** he or she sees in the situation in terms of possibilities of developing a counseling relationship.

The client must also assess the "cost" of an invitation. Typically, the person seeking out the counselor has learned that trust can and will be violated, and the would-be client must assess the risks and costs involved in accepting or rejecting an invitation from the counselor. Quite often the basic issue involved is the question: "Does the possibility of gain through counseling offset the risks and costs of engaging in a counseling relationship?" The response to this question will vary with the experiences and the perceptions each person brings to the counseling relationship, in addition to the way the person thinks he or she perceives the counselor. For the invited client, there are also a number of considerations in viewing the extended invitation. These might include: Why is this person even interested in me? (read: "What does he or she want?") What is in that invitation for me? What has my own experience been, related to others extending themselves to me? What do I possibly

Figure 1
A Modification of
Purkey's Anatomy of an Invitation

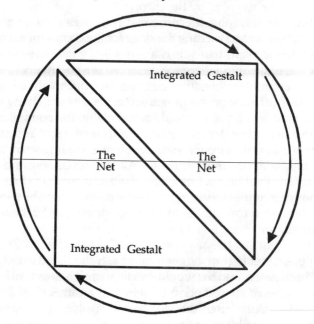

1. *Invitor's Perceptual Field Ground*
Sensitivity to stimuli concerning the client

Belief systems about self
    Feelings of efficacy as a counselor.   Feelings of value as a counselor.
    Feelings of relatedness to others.   Feelings of value as a person.
Belief systems about others
    Perceiving others to be: Worthy, able, valuable, and needing affirmation.
Belief systems about the world
    Basically stable, predictable, reliable, and supportive.
FIGURE
    Intention to invite; Commitment to invite; Timing; Risk-taking.

Figure 1 (continued)

2. *Invitor's Behavior: The Communicative Act*

Verbal	Non-verbal
Intended (responding intentionally)	Unintended (responding unintentionally)
Formal (counselor training)	Informal (counselor as a person)

Communication Skills:
Listening; Perceiving; Responding; Body language.

3. *Invitee's Perceptual Field Ground*
Sensitivity to stimuli concerning situation.

Belief Systems:
About self, about personal sense of efficacy, about personal worth and value.
Belief Systems:
About others' dependability and trustworthiness, and about one's world.
FIGURE:

Invitation recognized;	Risks involved;
Risks deemed appropriate;	Risks willing to accept.

4. *Invitee's Responding Behavior*

The Communicative Act:

Verbal	Non-verbal
Intended (responding intentionally)	Unintended (responding unintentionally)
Formal (expected responses)	Informal (spontaneous expressions)

Communicative Skills:
Listening; Perceiving; Responding; Body Language.

---

gain? What do I possibly lose? If I accept this initial offer, what is likely to follow? In other words, where the client **thinks** he or she stands determines what the client **thinks** he or she sees as possibilities in the counseling relationship.

A client recently told a counselor how difficult it was to trust after being hurt and disappointed too many times. In a session where the counselor and client were recapping what each perceived had taken place in their interactions, the client said:

At first I thought you would be like all the others

who said they cared about me and my concerns. But I saw them looking at their watches every five minutes or so, making sure the 50 minutes weren't up. You said you would be there with me when I needed you, and I had to test you. Remember those phone calls at 2:00 and 3:00 in the morning? You were there, and I came to depend upon that because you never let me down. You took me seriously, and because of that I was able to look at things I have never been able to tell anyone else. I knew you would stay with me. The others were phony, and I was beginning to believe there was nobody I could trust to hear me. I found myself pulling into myself more and more, thinking I would never take the risk of trusting another person or counselor again because they were too frightened by the things that really scared me. (Stafford, 1989, p. 4.)

Clearly, before extending an invitation to a client, the responsible counselor must ask if he or she is willing to expend the effort, energy, time, and commitment should the client accept the invitation extended, for an invitation carelessly extended may be harmful to both client and counselor.

It is assumed the inviting counselor is reasonably in touch with his or her own private perceptual field--i.e., the counselor's attitudes, values, views of the human condition; views of the counselor's strengths, and their limitations; views of the counselor's own energy levels; the counselor's pervasive perceptions of others; perceptions of risks involved for the counselor and his or her clients, etc. Returning to the prior notion of trust, does the counselor view his or her self as trustworthy in extending an invitation, and does the counselor also trust the other in terms of accepting or rejecting the invitation?

One of the most difficult issues for both neophyte and seasoned counselors is the counselor's ability to understand that rejection of an invitation in a counseling relationship is **not** a rejection of the counselor as either a professional or a person. Most typically, the client's rejection is a clear message that the client is unable, from his or her perceptual viewpoint, to trust one's self or the situation enough to accept the invitation. A client this guarded, however, is not likely to say, "no thank you, not at this time," for even that would make the person too vulnerable. As a result, the rejection typically appears unequivocal, and ofttimes harsh.

Intentionality

Intentionality has been viewed in a number of different ways in a counseling relationship. Rollo May (1969) described intentionality as "the structure which gives meaning to experience" (p. 223). Purkey and Schmidt (1987) added that: "He [May] viewed intentionality as the ability of people to link their inner consciousness and perceptions with their intentions and overt behaviors" (p. 52). In an attempt to clarify this further, May (1969) noted that intentionality "is not to be identified with intentions, but is the dimension which underlies them; it is man's [sic] capacity to have intentions" (p. 224).

Purkey (1978), Purkey and Novak (1984), and Purkey and Schmidt (1987) indicated that intentionality is a crucial dimension of the inviting process, and indeed, the two extremes of their inviting paradigm include both intentionally inviting as well as intentionally disinviting behaviors in human interactions. What is often overlooked, however, is that both of these dimensions share a commonality, for both are intentional acts. Purkey and Novak (1984) and Purkey and Schmidt (1987) stressed that while disinviting messages are not facilitative (indeed they are often lethal), an intentionally disinviting message may be more easily understood than an un-intentionally disinviting message or even an un-intentionally inviting message, since the un-intentional messages lack clear meaning, direction, or purpose.

Intentionality is viewed as a desired goal for an effective counseling relationship. However, the counselor who is **attempting** to be intentionally inviting and is not considering all the ramifications of the invitation being accepted, may find himself or herself in the awkward position of musing, "But that is not what I meant in extending that invitation, and I am uncomfortable with the responsibilities that come with that acceptance" (Stafford, 1989, p. 3). The potential for harm to both the client and the counselor exists when the counselor fails to examine carefully the ramifications of the invitation extended.

The intentionally inviting counselor, however, would attempt to consider the ramifications of his or her behaviors, especially including the consequences and responsibilities of any invitation being accepted. The issue of intentionality is not unique to invitational counseling, but it does hold particular prominence in the whole structure of the invitational model. It is perhaps more clearly exemplified in the modification of Purkey's anatomy of an invitation.

The Net

One of the major understandings found in Purkey's anatomy of an invitation lies in the gestalt net which separates the counselor from the client. The use of the net as an image in this paradigm is crucial in understanding the relationship of persons on both sides of the net, and, equally important, in understanding both behaviors and possible behaviors of individuals on either side of the net. Purkey and Schmidt (1987) refer to "honoring the net" when they state:

> The "net" is a hypothetical boundary between the
> counselor and the client that marks an inviolable
> territory for each. While self-disclosure should
> occur in a **trusting** [emphasis added] counseling

relationship, the client remains in control of what he or she will or will not disclose. This is as it should be....The inviter determines the rules under which invitations are sent; but the invitee determines the rules of acceptance....No matter how helpful the counselor desires to be, in invitational counseling the net is always respected. But honoring the net, [although] necessary, is not sufficient. Therefore, the next step of the inviting process is ensuring the invitation has been received. (p. 74)

The net serves as a useful metaphor in counseling. It is as if the net were a veil, albeit a thin veil, separating counselor and client. No matter how thin the veil, however, it serves the purpose of protecting the integrity of each, and it is only an act of intentional volition on the part of the client that allows the veil to be lifted temporarily, but seldom if ever completely removed.

This is perhaps most evident in counseling with young children, where play therapy is used as a medium of expression. In play therapy, for example with puppets, the child-client may allow him or herself to lift the veil partially by taking the risk to state what is important to be said, but with the recognition that he or she may also elect to retreat behind the net at any time the child becomes uncomfortable by using the guise of the statement coming from the puppet and not the child. In those situations where children may frighten themselves in terms of what they are doing or saying, and where they are not entirely comfortable with the issue of trust with the counselor, they will often suddenly retreat behind the net and disown what the puppet has said or done. This need to retreat to safety is important, for it allows the child to pace what it is he or she is trying to process. While this may be apparent with children, it is equally true with any client, regardless of age, in terms of honoring the net.

The client needs to be assured that he or she may partially lift the net if the client chooses to determine what risks may be involved in accepting or partially accepting an invitation. However, the client also needs the reassurance that he or she may retreat to safety behind the net, knowing the counselor will not attempt to violate the net nor the individual's integrity. The client must know that one may make oneself transparent and vulnerable on "the other side of the net" whenever he or she feels the time is appropriate and safe.

Inviting As a Dynamic Process

It is tempting and oversimplified to look at these above processes as being appropriate only at the initiation of a counseling relationship, when better judgment tells us instead that counseling is a dynamic and ongoing process. An inviting stance is not extended as an introduction to the counseling process only, but is a necessary attitude and process which is constantly sensitive, fluid, spontaneous, and dynamic in interacting with the client. This is based, in part, on skills and the perceptiveness of the counselor as noted previously, and it is also based on the perceptions and beliefs of the client. Each new interaction between counselor and client presents its own unique dynamics, and the nature of the interaction changes with each new transaction. In part, this is why such concepts as "establishing rapport" seem arcane, because the implication, and often the belief, is that once rapport has been established, it is an accomplished fact. Anyone who has engaged in the counseling process realizes this is not the case. Furthermore, rapport is not merely a one-way interaction from the counselor to the client. Instead, it is an **inter**active process between two individuals (i.e., counselor to client, and client to counselor), as well as an **intra**active process within the individual of the counselor or the client.

Perhaps an anecdotal account will help clarify this point. Recently, a counselor was working with a young man who was experiencing a great deal of isolation and loneliness, and who wanted, more than anything else, to be able to establish an intimate relationship with a young woman. The problem was that the young man genuinely wanted this kind of relationship, but believed that he was totally incapable of offering the intimate side of himself in such a relationship. Prior experiences had taught him to keep up his guard so that he would not get hurt in an encounter of the close kind.

Initially, he had difficulty developing trust with the counselor, who tried to read and understand the client's perceptual field, and in time the client appeared to come to trust the relationship as being genuine and safe. We might say that in this case the counselor had extended an invitation to join in a therapeutic bond, and the client had accepted. Mission accomplished? Hardly.

The next step was the counselor's attempt to move about in the client's world of understandings, feelings, and beliefs. The counselor attempted to assist the client to search inside himself in an attempt to become more intimate first with himself. Although the counselor perceived that he moved slowly, tried to read the client's perceptual field carefully, and to proceed cautiously, the client could deal with his inner self only in highly cognitive terms. Instead of allowing himself to experience himself, the client reported that he felt a strong need to "give tips to himself" so he could avoid future hurts.

The counselor had attempted to be sensitive not to violate the client's net, an issue upon which trust had originally been developed. However, both the counselor and the client recognized very much at the same time that they were probably at an impasse, and one which would probably inhibit further movement because of the client's anxiety in letting go of his cognitive and defensive posture. Consequently, both agreed that they were at a point of termination, which in fact occurred. While on the surface this may appear to be a colossal failure in counseling, some weeks later the counselor received a note from the client which read in part:

Just a quick note to say "thanks" for all of your
help and support during our sessions. It's truly
been a revealing and intriguing experience to
share some of my confusion, loneliness, and anxious sorrow with you. Unfortunately, I am not
used to sharing such intimate secrets and the
anxiety associated with revealing myself had become overwhelming. I'm sure that seems foreign
to you since you deal with it on a daily basis, but
I felt that I had reached my limit for now. Maybe
someday I can return....Thanks again for caring.
(Stafford, 1991)

In situations where trust is rather firmly established and the
therapeutic bond is developed between counselor and client, new
dimensions of interaction may take place. In such situations, the
counselor may be able to move about in the client's perceptual
world and, through careful and sensitive interaction, the counselor
may express, by reflection or confrontation, new insights or understandings to the client which the client previously had not been able
to accept or understand. Sheldon Kopp (1974) stated this vividly in
his description of Carl Rogers' contribution to the human potential
movement when he stated:

Rogers' own profound humanness, his incredible
gentleness, and his heart-rending concern make it
hard for me to listen to some of the tape recordings
of his work with clients without feeling tears
rising up behind my eyes. And, yet, I felt even
better about what Rogers was doing when, in later
years, he began to come across as someone who
helped others by being tough as well as tender.
(Kopp, 1974)

Kopp was referring to Rogers' skill at confronting his clients in
a therapeutic manner, a notion often not understood not only in
person-centered counseling, but a notion which may also seem

foreign to invitational theory. Patterson and Eisenberg (1983) viewed confrontation as a means of focusing "the client's attention on some aspect of his or her behavior that, if changed, would lead to more effective functioning" (p. 75). Cormier and Cormier (1985) stated the "purpose of confrontation is to help the client become more aware of discrepancies or incongruities in thoughts, feelings, and actions" (p. 118). In brief, the purpose of confrontation is an attempt to help the client achieve a sense of wholeness or congruence. Purkey and Schmidt (1987) acknowledged the value of confrontation, as well as the counselor's purpose and role in this area when they stated, "By emphasizing these [confrontational] skills, counselors are able to establish and maintain a dependable stance in being professionally inviting with others" (p. 97).

A Reconceptualization

Much has been written and will continue to be written about the place of invitational theory in counseling. The intent here has been to examine basic issues, theoretical and philosophical, of invitational theory with which to explore a counseling format.

The question still lingers: What is new in this theory? In a real sense there is nothing dramatically new that is not found in many existing counseling theories. Invitational theory is not intended as yet another theory for counseling practitioners to consider and master. Theorists and practitioners have indicated there are already both redundancies and contradictions in counseling theory, and an additional layer is not viewed with enthusiasm. Belkin (1988) addressed this issue:

> What the practicing counselor, bombarded by a plethora of theories and assumptions about personality often incompatible with each other, would probably do best to remember is Carl Gustav Jung's (1954) pointed injunction: "Learn your theories as well as you can, but put them aside when

you touch the miracle of the living soul." (p. 42)

What is unique about invitational theory has been stated earlier. Invitational theory is the context in which to consider the content of many counseling theories. Even when a counselor "knows" a counseling theory, without the proper context of the expression of the theory, the result may be mechanical and may run directly counter to what the counselor is attempting to achieve. The result may well be a cardboard imitation which bears little resemblance or understanding of the theoretical approach being embraced. Invitational theory is the consistent marker to the individual practitioner that there is **more than** knowing about a counseling theory and **more than** knowing about personality dynamics that are involved in the counseling process. Those writing about invitational theory often speak of taking an inviting stance. This term seems well chosen, for it is the stance that serves to bring together parts and pieces of the total gestalt of the counseling process. One is vividly reminded of the gestalt axiom that the whole does equal more than the sum of the parts, and perhaps this becomes more apparent when we consider the invitational stance as the epoxy which joins these pieces of theory and understandings together in yet a new configuration of the counseling process.

The invitational stance beckons us to re-frame, to re-examine, and to re-position ourselves in this counseling process in such a way the process becomes energized into a new and exciting reconfiguration. It is the stance that provides the opportunity for the individual counselor to look through a new lens at the counselor-client interactions, permitting the counselor a different perspective of these interactions. Indeed, Engel's (1987) admonishment of where you **think** you stand determines what you **think** you see adds an additional sense of clarity to the invitational perspective. While other theories and positions have attempted to address similar types of issues concerning counselor stance, none has done it perhaps with the captivating forcefulness and clarity of invitational theory.

This author respectfully disagrees with Purkey and Schmidt (1987) when they try to embrace a wide range of counseling theories under the general rubric of invitational theory. This appears to have resulted in a forced fit of some counseling theories which philosophically do not appear to correspond. In the broader context of invitational theory, Purkey and Schmidt (1987, p. 5) recognize this philosophical mismatch when they stated that in any human interaction we need to consider whether we are "doing with" a person (i.e., respect and believe the individual has the best understanding of a given situation in his or her life, and thereby has the capacity for the most effective resolutions to his or her concerns, but that the person needs another to hear the individual as he or she journeys along the way) or "doing to" a person (i.e., a belief the individual is not capable of resolving his or her issues, and, instead, needs the direct intervention of the more knowing counselor).

Obviously, invitational theory is a doing-with approach. Using the doing-with model, which clearly matches invitational theory, it becomes more apparent that not all counseling theories can comfortably fit under the invitational umbrella. Those counseling theories which do fit the doing-with approach, however, take on a richer and more meaningful understanding of both the theory and especially the practice of that theory when exercised within the context and the stance of invitational theory.

A Final Consideration

In concluding, let me tell you another story. Again, it is not my story, but it is a good story and a true story about a school district in New Jersey. It is an important story because it demonstrates the power of an inviting-type of school counselor who probably never even heard of invitational theory, but she knew how to practice it.

A school board was meeting for the busy end-of-the year

meeting with the school administrators. The year had been difficult, and the next year promised to be even more difficult because budget constraints were affecting programs in the school. One of the positions to be dropped, because of budgetary concerns, was the counselor for the Student Assistance Program, previously called the Substance Abuse Program. The name change reflected a growing concern in the community for adolescent suicide prevention.

The school district is not affluent; education does not appear to be highly valued within the community, and students seldom speak out on educational issues, perhaps because most issues seem too removed from their world. And, yet, a group of students had gathered awkwardly in the back of the room where the board was meeting. The superintendent acknowledged the students' presence and asked them if they had something they wished to say.

After a brief pause, several of the students began to speak at once: "We heard [counselor] was going to be fired....You can't take her away from us....None of us even wants to go to school if she's not here" (Savadove, 1991, p. 36) was their uneasy opening. They were all novices with this experience, as students in this district historically do not appear at board meetings, and neither students nor board members quite knew how they should respond to one another.

The superintendent tried to explain in a clear, logical manner about the budget shortfall, an increasing student population, and funds which were not increasing proportionately. Finally, one of the students mustered all the courage he had, and stated: "It's obvious you've made up your minds to say no to whatever we say. Why didn't you ask us? Isn't what we want important? Isn't that what school is all about?"

Said another student: "How are we going to..." she stopped, needing the right word "...deal...without her?"

The board president responded: "There was a school before her. There will be after..."

Said one student: "Before I met [counselor] I was a drug addict and an alcoholic. Now I am straight. What am I going to do now? Who am I going to talk to?"

The superintendent countered: "There are people we believe can carry on the work. If we're wrong, then you can come back next year and tell us."

Student: "Then it'll be too late." (Savadove, 1991, p. 36)

As the meeting continued on, with students speaking passionately and the adults logically, nerves were finally frayed. One student, in exasperation finally said: "So, you are just telling us there's nothing you are going to do about [counselor]..."

Superintendent: "Yes. That's right. We can't."

Student: "There's no such thing as can't."

Superintendent: "Look, attacking us doesn't help anything."

Student: "We don't mean to attack you. It's just that..."

Student: "You don't realize this...you don't realize this, but I'd be dead today if it wasn't [sic] for her." There was a pause, the kind that happens when a truth is recognized. (Savadove, 1991, p. 42)

One example obviously does not make a point, but the power of this example is commanding. A dialogue between adolescents, who were obviously not in the mainstream of the school, and school administrators and the school board had taken place. This in itself is remarkable that it even happened. What the outcome was, although important to both sides, is still not the major issue.

What is astonishing is that an unlikely group of students, who felt disconnected from much of the school, came together in an awkward attempt to convey that **someone** had convinced them they were important. **Someone** had invited them to join with her in an attempt to redefine themselves and the value of themselves and of their lives, even to the point of confronting the ultimate school authorities in their lives. One can only imagine the power and the skill of that counselor's invitations and the lasting effect she had on that group of young people. The ultimate invitation had been extended to at least one young person who spoke..."You don't realize this...you don't realize this, but I'd be dead today if it wasn't [sic] for her" (Savadove, 1991, p. 42). What an eloquent tribute to that counselor who had extended the ultimate invitation to live!

References

Belkin, G. S. (1988). *Introduction to counseling* (third edition). Dubuque, IA: Wm. C. Brown.

Cormier, W. H., & Cormier, L. S. (1985). *Interviewing strategies for helpers* (second edition). Monterey, CA: Brooks/Cole.

Engel, G. L. (Winter, 1987). Where you think you stand determines what you think you see. *The Pharos*, 50, 21-24.

Erikson, E. H. (1963). *Childhood and society*. New York: W. W. Norton.

Hamachek, D. E. (1985). The self's development and ego growth: Conceptual analysis and implications for counselors. *Journal of Counseling and Development*, 64, 136-142.

Kopp, S. G. (Speaker). (1974). Search for a new guru: The third force (Cassette Recording No. 3). Chicago, IL: Human Development Institute.

May, R. (1969). *Love and will*. New York: W. W. Norton.

Moustakas, C. E. (1972). *Loneliness and love*. New York: Prentice-Hall.

Patterson, L. E., & Eisenberg, S. (1983). *The counseling process* (third edition). Boston, MA: Houghton Miflin.

Purkey, W. W. (1978). *Inviting school success*. Belmont, CA: Wadsworth.

Purkey, W. W., & Novak, J. M. (1984). *Inviting school success* (second edition). Belmont, CA: Wadsworth.

Purkey, W. W., & Schmidt, J. J. (1987). *The inviting relationship: An expanded perspective of professional counseling*. Englewood Cliffs, NJ: Prentice-Hall.

Savadove, L. (1991, June 19). Student protest over fired teacher halts board meeting. *The Sandpaper*, 36 and 42.

Stafford, W. B. (1989, December). Are you sure you want to invite? *Lite-Invite Letter*, 10(4), 4-5.

Stafford, W. B. (1991). Observations from a counselor's notebook. Unpublished manuscript.

Wrenn, C. G. (1990). From counselor toward becoming a person: Some suggestions. *Journal of Counseling and Development*, 68, 586.

Chapter 11
Inviting Things To Do in the Privacy of Your Own Mind

By Paula Helen Stanley

The present chapter focuses on the influence of intrapersonal processes as they affect individual choice and decision. Hundreds of times a day, individuals choose whether or not to accept or refuse invitations. In choosing what invitations they will accept and refuse, human beings help create their own destiny. Quality of life is determined by the choices people make.

This chapter proposes that one intrapersonal characteristic, cognitive clarity, greatly influences individual choice. Cognitive clarity is characterized by the presence of healthy core assumptions, such as "I don't have to be perfect to be accepted," and "It is acceptable to show my emotions." Cognitive clarity is in contrast to cognitive distortions in thinking, which are based on faulty core assumptions (i.e., "I must be perfect to be accepted").

Internal dialogue or inner self-talk reflects one's degree of cognitive clarity. By examining internal dialogue, individuals can develop an awareness of cognitive distortions and faulty core assumptions they use in thinking and the intrapersonal processes that function to perpetuate them.

The context in which intrapersonal processes will be examined is that of invitational theory. Invitational theory (Purkey & Novak, 1984; Purkey & Schmidt, 1987) is concerned with the context of learning and living. One major concept of invitational theory relevant to the present discussion of intrapersonal process is that of intentionality. Intentionality of behavior and choice is based upon knowledge and the ability to perceive alternatives and multiple interpretations of life events. It requires flexibility in thought and more accurate perception of events. Four levels of intentionality will be discussed next.

Four Levels of Intentionality

Four levels of intentionality include: intentionally inviting, unintentionally inviting, unintentionally disinviting, and intentionally disinviting (Purkey & Novak, 1984; Purkey & Novak, 1988; Purkey & Schmidt, 1990; Purkey & Schmidt, 1987). Each level represents a mode of operation that consists of attitudes and behaviors. Intentionality indicates active and purposeful choice. Unintentionality in behavior indicates that people behave without adequate forethought or knowledge; they may not perceive the freedom to choose or may lack the commitment that it takes to be intentional in behavior. Whatever, the reason, unintentional behavior can be thought of as a boat without a rudder. It goes wherever the winds or tides direct it. Intentionality is like the rudder that would keep a crew going in the direction it would desire.

An explicit feature of intentionality is that humans always have a choice—intentionality is possible regardless of the situation. Viktor Frankl (1962; 1991) placed great emphasis on choice and intentionality in a vivid recollection of his experiences in a German prisoner of war camp during World War II. He described conditions that seem impossible to tolerate—extremely cold weather, severe physical abuse, lack of food, separation from his family, and constant threat of death by Nazi guards. In *Man's Search For Meaning* (1962), he described how he survived by intentionally making a choice to do just that—to survive. In *The Doctor and The Soul* (1955), Frankl described the freedom individuals have to choose how they will respond to a situation:

> For whatever may have been taken from them in their first hour in camp—until his last breath no one can wrest from a man [*sic*] his freedom to take one or another attitude toward his destiny. And alternative attitudes really did exist. Probably in every concentration camp there were individuals who were examples of renunciation and self-sacrifice. Asking nothing of themselves, they went about on the grounds and in the barracks of the camp, offering a kind word here, a last crust of bread there. (p. 97)

The ability of these prisoners to make choices about how to live in life-threatening situations was a matter of changing their thinking about the situation in which they found themselves. They actively searched to find meaning in their suffering rather than succumbing to an inhumane environment. The environment could not take from them their freedom to choose—to intentionally find meaning and purpose in their horrible situation. Although most individuals never have to face the type of situation described by Frankl, they can become more intentional in behavior to improve the quality of their lives.

There are four levels of intentionality described by Purkey and associates that have importance for the messages we send ourselves (Purkey & Novak, 1984; 1988; Purkey & Schmidt, 1987; 1990; Purkey & Stanley, 1991). Each is described below.

Intentionally Inviting

Being intentionally inviting with oneself means that we value ourselves as individuals with unique talents, abilities, and ideas. We believe that "we are enough." Because people value themselves, they find ways to discover and enhance who they are. They stay focused in the present, which includes setting goals and making plans for the future. They accept invitations to learn more, to enjoy friendships, and to follow special interests. Such individuals also continually pay attention to their needs and set limits that are healthy and in their best interests. They treat themselves with dignity. When a mistake is made, intentionally inviting persons do not call themselves "stupid" or "hopeless." They accept that they are human, correct the mistake if they can, and learn from it. Being intentionally inviting with ourselves means we know that we will not always know "the answer," and that we don't have to.

Some would suggest that it doesn't matter what people say to themselves. These individuals see nothing harmful in calling oneself "stupid" or "hopeless." Research in the area of internal dialogue by Meichenbaum (1977; 1985) and Beck and associates (1976; 1989) indicates that it does matter what we say to ourselves. What we say to ourselves is strongly related to depression, anxiety, loneliness, and performance in many areas (i.e., test-taking, giving speeches). Our internal dialogue is an intrapersonal process that reveals and perpetuates our belief in core assumptions that may be faulty.

Intentionality involves a concerted effort to monitor our own internal dialogue and determine the faulty core assumptions it reflects. It means that we speak to ourselves with respect and caring. We would expect no less from others. Could we expect less from ourselves? We also challenge faulty core assumptions, such as "I must be perfect in everything I do to be accepted."

Individuals who operate from the intentionally inviting level do not call themselves names, collect more information before they reach conclusions about something, and use reason as well as emotion in making decisions. They report fewer cognitive distortions in thinking.

Unintentionally Inviting

Being unintentionally inviting with ourselves means that most of the time we use few cognitive distortions in thinking. Because we are behaving unintentionally, however, we are easily sidetracked by events around us. When we are under stress or pressure or the scrutiny of others, we lose our direction and sense of purpose. At these moments, we become disinviting towards ourselves.

What makes our behavior unintentional is that we do not know the value of internal dialogue and how distortions in thinking can upset us. When we have not done as well as we would have liked, when our true love does not show us the affection we expected, and when the dishwasher quits working, we may slip into blaming ourselves for all of these "disasters" or take them as a sign that we are no longer loved. Learning about the significance of internal dialogue, common cognitive distortions, and faulty core assumptions can lead to greater intentionality in behavior.

Unintentionally Disinviting

In this case, the major stance towards ourselves is one of disrespect and condemnation, but it is unintentional. We do not plan to use negative self-talk. Because of past learning and experience, we may perceive ourselves as less worthy than others and think negative self-talk to be reasonable.

People who reason from this stance are probably not aware of their own internal dialogue or the faulty core assumptions underlying it. They may feel depressed, guilty, angry, or sad, and not know why. The may perceive themselves as the cause of others' difficulties, flawed because they are not perfect, or disliked because they misread the intentions of others.

A former student of mine demonstrated unintentionally disinviting behavior. She felt that expression of feelings was not acceptable, especially angry feelings. She was afraid if she expressed her anger, she would become a tyrant who would be out of control. In addition, when she felt angry, she experienced guilt and anxiety. Only through counseling did she become aware that having angry feelings is an aspect of being human, and that such feelings can be expressed in constructive ways. Because she no longer felt guilty and anxious about being angry, she began to truly value herself and became more self-accepting.

Intentionally Disinviting

Being intentionally disinviting with oneself may result from growing up in environments that are uncaring and destructive. Persons who are intentionally disinviting with themselves willfully and purposefully cause themselves harm and discomfort. They have most likely experienced physical and/or emotional abuse from others earlier in life. Individuals who grow up in abusive environments often continue to abuse themselves in the same harmful manner as others have treated them previously. People who are intentionally disinviting with themselves most often need assistance from helping professionals to overcome their sense of worthlessness and to interrupt a pattern of self-abuse.

As can be seen in the example of intentionally disinviting behavior, intentionality may be used in the service of causing harm. Knowledge and certain attitudes and beliefs are important in guiding one's intentionality. In the case of intrapersonal intentionality, a knowledge of the significance of internal dialogue and the influence of core assumptions as they affect behavior is essential.

Internal Dialogue

Internal dialogue refers to the ongoing self-talk that takes place within an individual's mind (Meichenbaum, 1977). We are constantly having conversations with ourselves about the meaning and significance of events that take place in our daily lives. We think, "Did I do that OK? What if they didn't like it? What if they don't ask me to play again. Maybe they are afraid to tell me the truth. No one ever listens to me. But maybe I did OK. Nobody laughed or left the room. Yeah, I think I did OK." We have dialogues with ourselves in which we may debate, criticize, or congratulate our efforts.

A major focus of many cognitive theorists has been the structure and function of internal dialogue. Internal dialogue may be task-focused, self-focused, or relate to events beyond one's present environment. It may contain strategies, reassurances of the appropriateness of one's behavior, or evaluative comments which may be positive or negative. In general, internal dialogue is under the control of the individual, and can be used to alter one's emotional state or behavior. Substantial research has shown that internal dialogue may influence one's experience of anxiety, assertiveness, depression, and performance in many areas (Freeman, Simon, Beutler, & Arkowitz, 1989; Kendall & Hollan, 1981; Stanley, 1991).

Studies in the area of test anxiety (Edelmann & Hardwick, 1986; Hunsley, 1987; Mikulincer, 1989; Minor & Gold, 1986; Ottens, Tucker, & Robbins, 1989) have shown that one's internal dialogue can have either a debilitative or facilitative effect on test performance. High speech anxiety has been associated with internal dialogue characterized by cognitive distortions (Meichenbaum, 1977). Poor performance was associated with self statements that emphasized danger in the situation and fear of evaluation of others.

Internal dialogue which contains negative self-statements may become habitual and lead to self-defeating patterns of behavior. Negative self-statements are associated with depression in normal and clinical populations (Beck, 1976). Depressed individuals often criticize themselves subvocally. Events are misinterpreted, and one reinforces this biased view with negative self-statements. An example of a negative self-statement is, "I'm so unattractive, no one could like me."

In Beck's theory of depression, negative self-statements are neither logical nor valid. Beck proposes that automatic thoughts, one type of self-statement, are at the root of depression. Automatic thoughts are contained within one's "stream of thought," and often are out of one's awareness (Beck, 1976; Kendall & Hollan, 1981). Automatic thoughts are not the result of reason or reflection. They have an involuntary quality which encourages a depressed person to believe them to be an accurate reflection of reality.

Underlying one's internal dialogue are core assumptions that are basic beliefs individuals use to understand and interpret life events. They may be faulty (maladaptive) or adaptive. The significance of core assumptions has been the cornerstone of many cognitive theorists and can be found in the teachings of ancient philosophers, such as Epictetus (Long, 1890), who stated, "Men [sic] are disturbed not by the things which happen, but by the opinions about the things" (p. 381).

Core Assumptions

Albert Ellis (1962, 1982, 1985) and Aaron T. Beck (1976; 1989) are two psychologists who have developed the concept of beliefs as an influence on individual behavior. Each of them has developed a theoretical orientation which can be used to understand the power core assumptions can have on behavior. Ellis termed his beliefs "irrational ideas." Beck contributed the term "core assumptions" to refer to the belief system of an individual.

Irrational Ideas

Ellis, the founder of rational-emotive therapy, formulated a list of irrational ideas or assumptions which he believed caused all psychological disturbances. He developed an **A-B-C-D** paradigm to represent how events, beliefs, and consequences are related

(Ellis, 1982; 1985).

Irrational ideas are contained within one's belief system (**B**), which influences one's interpretation of an activating event (**A**). Ellis proposed that the consequences of interpreting an event using irrational ideas leads to a consequence (**C**) of being upset, with the attendant emotions of anger, sadness, or fear.

Examples of irrational ideas include "I must be competent in everything I do," "Others must treat me the way I want them to," "Things must turn out the way I want or I have to be upset," and "Everyone I consider important in my life must always approve of everything I do."

The solution used to decrease the likelihood of becoming upset is to actively dispute (**D**) the irrational ideas. This is done by examining the logic and probability of irrational ideas. By disputing irrational ideas, one alters one's belief system (Ellis, 1985).

An example of the A-B-C-D paradigm follows:

> A=**Activating event**: You oversleep and are late for work.
>
> B=**Belief system**: "I must be perfect to be accepted by others" and "I must always be accepted by others."
>
> C=**Consequences**: Guilt, fear, anxiety.
>
> D=**Dispute**: "It is regrettable that I was late for work, but I don't have to be perfect to be accepted by others. I made a mistake and I will be more careful next time. I am only human."

Beck's Information Processing Model

Beck (1976) proposed that thoughts are based on specific assumptions and premises that guide one's interpretation of environmental events. These assumptions and premises are based on past learning. They represent how one conceptualizes the world and one's self. "They shape perceptions into cognitions, formulate goals and values, provide interpretation, and assign meanings to events" (Beck & Weishaar, 1989, pp. 28-29). Some assumptions are core beliefs, which are the most stable of cognitive structures. They are discovered through inference from what a person says and how he or she behaves.

Some of the assumptions individuals hold are faulty and lead to erroneous conclusions (Beck, 1976; Beck & Weishaar, 1989). Examples of faulty core assumptions include: "People will probably think less of me if I make a mistake," "People should have a reasonable likelihood of success before undertaking anything," "I should be upset if I make a mistake," "If you don't have other people to lean on, you are bound to be sad," and "If I don't set the highest standards for myself, I am likely to end up a second-rate person" (Beck, 1976; Weissman, 1980).

Faulty core assumptions revolve around three major issues: acceptance, competence, and control (Beck, Emery, & Greenberg, 1985). These assumptions are activated when one encounters a stressor that is related to major concern, such as evaluation from a significant other. When faulty core assumptions are activated, they block new learning by altering one's information processing.

Faulty core assumptions cause one to process information so that one attends to certain features of the environment and ignores others. A person who is anxious attends only to danger in situations. A person who tends to be depressive focuses on what he or she may lose or his or her inadequacy.

Core assumptions which are learned and acted upon repeatedly lead to habitual behavior. By observing one's own behavior, one can infer what assumptions underlie his or her actions. We tend to repeat the same behavior patterns throughout our lives (Beck, Emery, & Greenberg, 1985; Mahoney & Freeman, 1985).

Beck proposed that during periods of distress, individuals shift to a "more primitive information-processing system" which is associated with "systematic errors in reasoning" (Beck & Weishaar, 1989, p. 23). These errors in reasoning are called cognitive distortions. Cognitive distortions used when faulty core assumptions are activated include overgeneralizing, all-or-none thinking, and emotional reasoning. Cognitive distortions lead to reduced risk-taking and defensiveness in behavior.

Cognitive Distortions

Many cognitive distortions have been identified by Beck (1988), Meichenbaum (1985), and others in the field of cognitive psychology. A strong correlation has been found among these cognitive distortions and behaviors such as depression, social anxiety, test anxiety, performance anxiety, submissiveness, and loneliness (Beck, 1976; 1988; Bruch, Kaflowitz, & Kuethe, 1986; Burns, 1982; Edelmann & Hardwick, 1986; Harrell & Ryon, 1983; Kendall & Hollon, 1989; Meichenbaum 1985; Minor & Gold, 1986). It is through identifying and challenging these distortions that one becomes more intentional in behavior and less controlled by thoughts of which one is unaware.

Cognitive distortions which have been identified include all-or-none thinking, overgeneralization, mental filtering, mind-reading, fortune-telling, magnification, emotional reasoning, "should" statements, labeling, personalization, blaming, catastrophizing, and double jeopardy. Each of these distortions will be discussed. Following the description of the distortions, techniques for challenging them will be presented.

All-or-None Thinking

An individual who reasons from an all-or-none stance perceives only two choices. Things appear to be one way or another. People like you or they don't. You think you are a success or a failure. There is a right answer and a wrong answer. This type of reasoning leads to the feeling that one must be perfect. Mistakes are not seen as opportunities to learn or a human characteristic that is unavoidable. Mistakes are seen as evidence of inadequacy. The use of words like never, always, need, must, and should indicate all-or-none thinking.

Overgeneralization

One makes an overall assumption based on one small piece of information. You think if something happened once, it will happen again with certainty. If one marriage didn't turn out well, a second one won't either. If you are not invited to a party, you may conclude, "Nobody likes me." Or you might think you will never learn how to sing, if not selected for the chorus. Words that are associated with overgeneralization include all, every, and everybody.

Mental Filtering

You select one small detail out of a situation that supports fears about your own inadequacies and ignore all other information. You see only certain aspects of a situation. You focus on the one negative comment someone made and not the ten positive ones that were received the same day. You look for signs of disapproval and overlook evidence of liking from others. Words associated with this type of reasoning include terrible, awful, disgusting, and horrendous.

Mind Reading

This type of reasoning is fantasy. You believe you know what others are thinking about you. Usually you assume what others are thinking is negative. If your employer frowns, you may assume it is a sign of disapproval when it may be an outward manifestation of pain associated with indigestion or a bad back.

Another aspect of mind reading is the use of the defense

mechanism, projection. You often project your own unacceptable wishes, attitudes, and feelings onto others—like a projector throwing an image on a blank screen. If you are mad at or disappointed in yourself, you may think others in your environment feel angry at or disappointed in you. If you are judgmental and critical of yourself, you may perceive others as being judgmental and critical of you. After all, you believe you can read others' minds.

Fortune Telling

You think you know for certain what will happen in the future. You assume that if certain behaviors are tried, the consequences will be unquestionable. You may think, "If I try skiing, I know I will break a leg." A female may assume that if she were three inches taller, more men would ask her out.

Magnification

This type of reasoning results in "blowing things way out of proportion." You overestimate the significance of an event. A new employee at a company may feel that his job is at stake if he comes in five minutes late one day. You hear a statement and make more of it than was meant. You may become upset because your spouse did not comment on the quality of food served at dinner. You perceive this lack of comment about the food to be a negative evaluation. You may not consider that your spouse is preoccupied or insensitive to your needs.

Emotional Reasoning

This type of cognitive distortion involves using what you feel to determine what is the truth about a situation. You do not use rational input—thinking, logic—to deduce the significance of an event or what you are feeling. If you feel like a failure, it is proof that you are a failure. If you feel angry, it is proof that someone has harmed you. If you feel inadequate, you are inadequate. The intensity of emotions involved in emotional reasoning acts as a barrier to more realistically assessing the facts in a situation. Use of consistent, frequent rational self-statements are useful in breaking the hold that emotional reasoning can have on us.

"Should" Statements

"Should" statements can be seen as residue from early childhood. Individuals who use many "should" statements operate from an external locus of control rather than internal locus of control. Their sense of worth and value is dependent upon what significant others think and feel about them. To behave or even think in a manner that is different from these significant others can cause a great deal of anxiety and uncertainty.

Individuals who use "should" statements assume there is an inflexible set of absolute rules by which they (and others) should live. Words often heard by individuals who use "should" thinking include must, ought, and have to. They may say "I shouldn't feel this way," "I should have known better."

Using should thinking can result in feelings of guilt and shame. This type of thinking also is associated with perfectionistic behavior. We limit ourselves by enforcing standards of behavior which are unrealistic and prevent us from developing much of the potential we have.

Labeling

Labeling is a type of cognitive distortion in which we make global statements about others and ourselves. We call ourselves or others names, such as "fool," "loser," "wimp," or "failure." Such name-calling can be harmful in that individuals may behave in ways that are consistent with labels given them.

This type of distortion also refers to making broad generalizations about others. One may call all men "insensitive and uncaring" or all women "overemotional and unstable." All students from a particular residential area may be called "trouble-makers."

Personalization

When one uses this type of cognitive distortion, one believes he or she is responsible for other people's moods and actions. We see everything as related to ourselves. It is our fault that it is raining. If someone we care about is mad or sad, we assume we did something to cause them to feel that way. If the school play did not turn out well, we take responsibility for that, too.

Another aspect of personalization is comparing oneself with others. We compare our qualities, traits, talents, and abilities with others. Comparing ourselves with others is not at all rational, because each of us is unique with our own life path to follow. By comparing ourselves with others, we are always in an inferior position. One can end the comparing by focusing on one's own personal growth and development in the context of one's own life.

Blaming

Individuals who reason from this type of thinking see others as the source of their problems. Other people create the problems and we do not see our contribution to the difficult situation. Statements emerging from this type of reasoning include "If it wasn't for him, everything would be fine" or "They messed it up for everyone."

To overcome this type of reasoning requires looking at one's own contribution to the situation. We can examine how we behaved by asking others for feedback. Those in the habit of blaming might find feedback from others threatening. Care must be taken to give sensitive and constructive feedback to individuals who reason in this manner.

Catastrophizing

Using catastrophizing is an effective way to increase one's anxiety quickly and efficiently. It involves expecting that the worst scenario will occur. We focus on the terrible and horrible things that can happen. We use "what if" statements. Statements often heard include, "What if I blow it?" "What if I faint?" "What if I forget what I was going to say?" "What if they don't like me?" "What if I don't do it well enough?"

"What if" statements block one from considering possible positive outcomes of behavior. We focus on the disasters that will surely occur as the result of trying something new or unknown. Such thinking may lead to a state of panic. As the result of catastrophizing, we may shy away from trying new things.

Double Jeopardy

Some individuals become aware of their distorted thinking and then punish themselves for this thinking. They become judgmental of their own distorted thinking. They feel guilt, anger, or shame because they have discovered one or more of the above types of distorted thinking. They then blame themselves for making "should" statements or using all-or-none thinking. Being critical of ourselves for thinking in a distorted manner is inhumane and disinviting. Becoming aware of distorted thinking we use is the first step to overcoming such thinking. It takes courage and persistence to achieve that awareness. Such courage and persistence deserves our respect, not our disparagement.

Cognitive distortions work in combination with each other. Where one can be identified, there are others involved as well. After identifying the distortions we use in thinking, we can learn to challenge or dispute them. In disputing and challenging these distortions, we can become more intentional in behavior. Our behavior is guided by knowledge of our wishes, knowledge of interpersonal relationships, and reason.

It takes patience and persistence to change our thinking. If we are willing to put forth the effort, the rewards are well worth it. The result is to be more in control of our thinking, feeling, and behaving. We are in the position to truly choose our actions and quality of life. Ideas useful for challenging and disputing cognitive distortions will be presented next.

Inviting Things To Do in the Privacy of One's Mind

Developing an awareness of cognitive distortions in thinking and then working to change those distortions are inviting acts that affect not only the individual but also those with whom that person lives and works. It is an invitation to be more caring and valuing of oneself, which is necessary to be caring and valuing of others. There are several inviting things one can do in the privacy of one's own mind to development an awareness of and change cognitive distortions in thinking (Beck, 1988; Burns, 1990; Ellis, 1985):

> 1. **Be an avid listener.** Listen carefully to the words you say, your inner thoughts, and how you feel. You can learn to identify faulty thinking by referring to the list of cognitive distortions presented earlier in this chapter.

> 2. **Separate fact from fiction.** Consider what evidence there is to support what you think. Consider the likelihood of a feared event actually occurring if you try something new. This may involve reading to increase your knowledge about the feared event or activity. You may find the percentage of airplanes that crash in a year, for

example. You may ask a ski resort manager how
many people actually break a leg each year.

3. **Treat yourself with the same respect you give
others.** Most of us consider it inhumane to call
others names or discourage them from trying to
learn and achieve. Yet, we may call ourselves
names and discourage ourselves in a very harsh
manner. For example, you might say, "I'm a failure." It is not likely that you will call someone else
a failure. You might say, "I couldn't do this math."
It is not likely you would tell someone else that he
or she couldn't do this math. Although we may go
to great lengths to avoid commenting on someone
else's potential, we are often careless with our
assessment of ourselves.

4. **Test your assumptions—Be a scientist.** If you
think something bad will happen if you try a new
behavior, try it and see. If you think a fellow
employee never likes your ideas and it is important to you for this person to like some of your
ideas, tell that person a lot of your ideas. If he or
she likes just one, you have disproved your assumption. (You have also learned that you can
handle rejection.) If you think you always forget
what you are going to say when you get up in front
of a group, try it a few times. If you did not forget
what you were going to say, at least one time, you
have disproved your assumption.

5. **Use the reframe.** Usually you can find something positive in a situation even if much of if is
unpleasant or disagreeable. Even if you forget a

couple of things you were going to say in front of the PTA, you presented the rest of the material well. You were also committed enough to participate in the meeting.

6. **Embrace relativity.** Using words like never and always is extreme. There are very few extremes or absolutes in life. Look for the shades of gray and the exceptions. Doing so results in a more humane evaluation of yourself and others.

7. **Be a detective.** Look at all of the evidence. If you feel like you are to blame for something, for example, look for other factors which may have made a contribution. Who else may have had an influence? What policies may have been at work? What other events may have had an influence on the situation?

8. **Check your perceptions.** Check your perceptions with others. What do they think about what you think? Do they think you are being too hard on yourself? Do others think you are overlooking some positive aspects of the situation? Do they perceive the situation in a similar way?

9. **Alter self-talk.** Many people believe that some self-talk perpetuates distorted thinking. By altering distorted self-talk, you are making a commitment to be more inviting with yourself. By intentionally monitoring your self-talk, you can become aware of habitual patterns of distorted thinking. In altering the self-talk, you begin to challenge distorted core assumptions.

Conclusion

Intentionality in behavior is an essential aspect of being human. According to invitational theory, intentionality is essential for our well-being and that of others. It places a high priority on human choice. The ability to choose, however, is not seen by everyone as an exciting possibility. Many people feel safer by letting others make their choices for them. They may be intentional in behavior, but they behave from others' beliefs systems. It is contingent upon the individual to choose the values and beliefs from which he or she behaves.

The premise of this chapter is that it is important for one to become aware of his or her core assumptions and internal dialogue in order to be intentionally inviting with self and others. An individual's internal dialogue and core assumptions are major factors that determine how one interprets the actions of self and others. This interpretation is the basis one uses to determine consequent actions. The consequent actions lead to behaviors which culminate in an interaction and an evaluation of that interaction.

By developing an understanding of internal dialogue and core assumptions, one can better understand one's own behavior and that of others. With this understanding, there is a greater awareness of how one's perceptual processes influence the categorization of experience and one's actions that are based on that categorization. When we choose a behavior, it is based on knowledge of self, understanding of others, a healthy degree of cognitive clarity, and the temperance needed to deal with ambiguity and uncertainty. Quality of life is enhanced as we help create our own life possibilities.

References

Beck, A. T. (1976). *Cognitive therapy and the emotional disorders.* New York: New American Library.

Beck, A. T. (1988). *Love is never enough.* New York: Harper & Row.

Beck, A. T., Emery, G., & Greenberg, R. (1985). *Anxiety disorders and phobias: A cognitive perspective.* New York: Basic Books.

Beck, A. T., & Weishaar, M. (1989). Cognitive therapy. In Freeman, A., Simon, K., Beutler, L., & Arkowitz, H. (editors), *Comprehensive handbook of cognitive therapy,* (21-36). New York: Plenum.

Bruch, M., Kaflowitz, N., & Kuethe, M. (1986). Beliefs and the subjective meanings of thoughts; Analysis of role of self-statements in academic test performance. *Cognitive Therapy and Research.,* 10, 51- 69.

Burns, D. D. (1982). Hope and hopelessness: A cognitive approach. In Abt, L. E., & Stuart, I. R. (editors), *The new therapies: A sourcebook,* (pp. 33-59). New York: VanNostrant Reinhold.

Burns, D. D. (1990). *The feeling good handbook.* New York: Plume.

Edelmann, R., & Hardwick, S. (1986). Test anxiety, past performance and coping strategies. *Personality and Individual Differences, 7,* 255-257.

Ellis, A. (1962). *Reason and emotion in psychotherapy.* Secauscas, NJ: Lyle Stuart & Citadel Books.

Ellis, A. (1982). *A guide to personal happiness.* North Hollywood, CA: Wilshire Books.

Ellis, A. (1985). Expanding the ABC's of Rational Emotive Therapy. In Mahoney, M. J., & Freeman, A. (editors), *Cognition and psychotherapy,* (313-324). New York: Plenum.

Frankl, V. (1955). *The doctor and the soul.* New York: Knopf.

Frankl, V. (1962). *Man's search for meaning: An introduction of logotherapy.* New York: Washington Square Press.

Frankl, V. (1991). From concentration camp to psychotherapist. Presentation to the Evolution of Psychotherapy Conference, Anaheim, CA.

Freeman, A., Simon, K., Beutler, L., & Arkowitz, H. (editors). (1989). *Comprehensive handbook of cognitive therapy.* New York: Plenum Press.

Harrell, T. H., & Ryon, N. B. (1983). Cognitive-behavioral assessment of depression: Clinical validation of the Automatic Thoughts Questionnaire. *Journal of Consulting and Clinical Psychology.* 51, 721-725.

Hunsley, J. (1987). Internal dialogue during academic examinations. *Cognitive Therapy and Research, 11*, 653-664.

Kendall, P. C., & Hollon, S. (editors). (1981). *Assessment strategies for cognitive-behavioral interventions.* New York: Academic.

Long, G. (1890). *The discourses of Epictetus; with the encheiridion and fragments.* London, England: George Bell and Sons.

Mahoney, M., & Freeman, A. (editors) (1985). *Cognition and psychotherapy.* New York: Plenum.

Meichenbaum, D. (1977). *Cognitive-behavior modification: An integrated approach. New* York: Plenum.

Meichenbaum, D. (1985). *Stress-inoculation training.* New York: Pergamon.

Mikulincer, M. (1989). Cognitive interference and learned helplessness: The effects of off-task cognitions on performance following unsolvable problems. *Journal of Personality and Social Psychology, 57*, 129-135.

Minor, S., & Gold, S. (1986). Behavior of test anxious students across time. *Personality and Individual Differences, 7*, 241-242.

Owens, A., Tucker, K., & Robbins, S. (1989). The construction of an academic anxiety coping scale. *Journal of College Student Development, 30*, 249-256.

Purkey, W. W., & Novak, J. M. (1984). *Inviting school success.* Belmont, CA: Wadsworth.

Purkey, W. W., & Novak, J. M. (1988) *Education: By invitation only.* Bloomington, IN: Phi Delta Kappa Fastback Series.

Purkey, W. W., & Schmidt, J. J. (1987). *The inviting relationship.* Englewood Cliffs, NJ: Prentice-Hall.

Purkey, W. W., & Schmidt, J. J. (1990). *Invitational learning for counseling and development.* Ann Arbor, MI: ERIC/CAPS.

Purkey, W. W., & Stanley, P. H. (1991). *Invitational teaching, learning, and living.* Washington, DC: National Education Association.

Stanley, P. H. (1991). Asymmetry in internal dialogue, core assumptions, valence of self-statements and counselor trainee effectiveness. Unpublished dissertation. University of North Carolina at Greensboro.

Weissman, A. N. (1980). Assessing depressogenic attitudes: A validation study. Paper presented at the 51st Annual Meeting of the Eastern Psychological Association, Hartford, CT.

Synthesis

Chapter 12
Reconceptualizing Invitational Thinking

By John M. Novak

In what ways has this volume deepened invitational thinking and its application to other areas of research and practice? By systematically looking at some issues raised and practices promoted in each of the chapters and recent rethinking of invitational education by the International Alliance for Invitational Education, we can see how this theory of invitational practice is deepened and made more coherent, vital, and interesting. Let us begin with the personal and move through the interpersonal, curricular, and organizational as we make our way to larger societal issues.

At the personal level, William Watson Purkey shows how an understanding of the phenomenology and structure of the self is vital for the inviting process. An informed feel for how people make sense of themselves and possibilities for change is essential for invitational educators. Without this deeper concern for the way life is lived from the inside out, inviting runs the risk of becoming a mechanical process done for external purposes. Adding to this deeper concern for the person in the process, Paula Helen Stanley explains how this informed feel must also be applied to ourselves.

The strategies she offers for removing cognitive distortions get us in touch with the various ways, seemingly rational and irrational, we all use to maintain, protect, and enhance our self-concept. This making sense of ourself and our situations is a highly personal and cognitive process. Perhaps it can be said, then, if you really want to get an understanding for inviting other people, pay attention to how you invite yourself. Each person is his or her own laboratory and project for coming to grips with the inviting perspective.

In paying attention to how we invite others, William B. Stafford points out the importance of attending to who we are and what we are about as we interact. Since trust is such an important part of an inviting relationship, the deeper dimensions of our intentionality need to be examined from our own perspective and the perceived perspective of those with whom we work. To be able to sustain an inviting relationship, each of has to be authentically trustworthy. This means that we have to be understood by others and be perceived as sincere, caring, competent, and appropriate. Thus, these details of trustworthiness are the "stuff" of inviting relationships. As Charlotte Reed cogently argues, this becomes particularly important as we work with people from different backgrounds. Here, the necessity for constructing relationships that support trust and that trust support is a *sine qua non*. But here also, issues of understanding, sincerity, caring, and appropriateness are often most fragile. Some case studies that show positive exemplars of the development of supportive relationships in multicultural settings would be a vital addition to an understanding of the inviting process.

However, support, although a necessary beginning, is not enough if we want to invite educative events. In looking at issues of cognitive development, Dorothy S. Russell points out the necessity for challenge in order to move beyond our present stage. The judicious use of constructive mismatch is an essential part of inviting development and an inviting curriculum. Development and curriculum are not about keeping things as they are; they both seek worthwhile movement in deeper, more integrated directions. This deeper, more integrated movement is demonstrated in the curricular changes suggested by cooperative education (Lisa Marie Beardsley and George M. Jacobs), physical education (John Kearns), and multicultural education (Charlotte Reed). Each of these curricular changes challenges traditional practices and calls for more responsive ways of teaching. The world is changing rapidly. We cannot stand still. But in order to move in inviting ways, we have to move in ways that are inviting. This is not tautological, but merely a way of emphasizing that inviting goals need to be pursued in inviting ways, because what you end up with is a culmination of the processes used. This is particularly true in administrative issues.

More innovative and responsive ways of teaching require administrative support and inviting structures if they are to be maintained, protected, and enhanced. That is why the Inviting Teaching Observation Instrument (ITOI) and the Teacher Improvement Process (TIP) developed by John Van Hoose and David Strahan are so important. They provide defensible, structured ways to call forth inviting teaching practices and develop inviting supervisory procedures. However, in order for inviting practices and procedures to be sustained, an inviting school culture must be established. It is in this light that the work of Dean Fink and Betty L. Seigel takes on additional meaning. The former provides a systematic way to understand inviting change while the latter gives a living example of inviting change in action. Both show the administrative intentionality and know-how necessary for developing and sustaining inviting change.

Change, however, needs a foundation if it is to be more than mere movement. It is here that the deeper societal commitments of invitational education come forth. Invitational thinking depends on and seeks to develop caring, reflective practitioners with the know-how and persistence necessary to develop, structure, and sustain educational environments that dependably call forth the worthwhile possibilities of all participants. This is its intentionality. This is also deeply connected to the intentionality of a democratic society envisioned by John Dewey. For Dewey, democracy was not merely a political form, but an ideal for communicative living that affirmed the worth, dignity, and possibilities of each person and necessitated the creation of forms of life that supported this ideal.

The relationship between this notion of democracy and the commitments of invitational educators can be noted in a recent draft of a mission statement by the International Alliance for Invitational Education. Here the connection has been made explicit. Because a democratic society is committed to the care and growth of all of its citizens, and because it depends on and values participation, and because the process is the product in the making, it follows that developing intentionally inviting people, places, policies, and programs is a way to put into practice these democratic ideals. Thus, invitational thinking is grounded in democratic ideals and leads to democratic practices.

Perhaps the next important move for invitational thinkers will be to attend to the people who have been traditionally excluded from meaningful participation in this democratic ideal. This is the point raised by Reed about multicultural participation and Beardsley and Jacobs about feminist thought. Inviting, like democracy, is not about intentionally or unintentionally sustaining monoculturalism, sexism, isolationism, or impoverished life possibilities. It is about plurality, equality, communication, and hopeful possibilities. In order to live up to these democratic commitments, invitational thinkers will have to closely examine places, programs, and policies in terms of their ability to seriously call forth the uniqueness and abilities of all of its citizens within and outside of schools. This will entail a continued thoughtful turn to ethical and political issues. Here is the challenge. Is there support?

Information
about the Contributors

Lisa Marie Beardsley was born in England to a Japanese American and a Finnish national. She has lived throughout the United States, and in England, Finland, Sweden, and the Philippines. She holds degrees in theology (B.Th.), health education (M.P.H.), and educational psychology (Ph.D.). She is currently Assistant Dean and on the faculty in Psychiatry and Behavioral Medicine at the University of Illinois College of Medicine at Peoria.

Dean Fink has been an administrator in both elementary and secondary schools, and is presently Superintendent of Instructional Services with the Halton Board of Education, Burlington, Ontario. He has made presentations, conducted workshops, and presented papers to educators across North America as well as in Europe and Israel. His publications on school effectiveness, change theory, and invitational education have been published in journals in Canada, the United States, and Europe.

George M. Jacobs holds degrees in political science (B.A.), Linguistics/English as a Second Language (M.A.), and Educational Psychology (Ph.D.). He has been an English as a Second Language teacher in the United States, Costa Rica, Nicaragua, China, and Thailand. He is currently teaching English at McKinley High School in Honolulu, Hawaii, and a course in cooperative learning at the University of Hawaii at Manoa.

John Kearns is Assistant Professor of Education with the Faculty of Education, Brock University, St. Catharines, Ontario. He has taught Physical Education at all levels ranging from primary to secondary and university. He is actively involved as a course conductor with the National Coaching Association of Canada.

John M. Novak is a Professor of Education and former Chair of Graduate Studies in Education at Brock University, St. Catharines, Ontario. He is co-author of *Inviting School Success* and *Education: By Invitation Only*. He has also published in the *International Journal of Personal Construct Psychology*, the *Journal of Education*, and *Interchange*. In addition, he is editor of *Insights*, a publication of the John Dewey Society.

William Watson Purkey is a Professor of Counselor Education at the University of North Carolina at Greensboro and co-director of the International Alliance of Invitational Education. He is the recipient of numerous awards for outstanding teaching and has published more than 80 articles and five books, including *Self-Concept and School Achievement* and *Inviting School Success*, co-authored with John M. Novak.

Charlotte Reed (Ed.D., The University of Virginia) is an Associate Professor of Education at Purdue University, Calumet, Indiana. She has been a teacher, teacher educator, and project director in public and private urban educational settings. She is an active consultant to school districts, colleges, universities, and government and private agencies.

Dorothy S. Russell is Director of Teacher Education and Graduate Programs at Salem College, Winston Salem, North Carolina. She is on several state advisory commissions in North Carolina.

Betty L. Siegel has been President of Kennesaw State College in Marietta, Georgia, since 1981. During that time, enrollment has risen dramatically from 4,000 to 11,000 students, and Kennesaw State has been named two years in a row by the *U. S. News and World Report* as one of the nation's "up-and-coming" regional colleges. A nationally known lecturer and consultant, Siegel has served as Chair of the Board of Directors of the American Association of State Colleges and Universities, and she is also co-founder and co-director of the International Alliance for Invitational Education.

William B. Stafford is currently Associate Professor of Counseling in the College of Education at Lehigh University, Bethlehem, Pennsylvania. Previously, he has been a resident counselor at Ohio and DePauw Universities, a school counselor and director of pupil services in Indiana, and a consultant to schools and state departments of education. He is also a counselor in private practice.

Paula Helen Stanley is Assistant Professor of Counseling and Development at Radford University, Radford, Virginia. She is an active writer and researcher, and has been published in the *Journal for Counseling and Development, Consortium for Whole Brain Learning,* and *Journal of the North Carolina Personnel and Guidance Association,* in addition to co-authoring *Invitational Teaching, Learning, and Living.*

Phyllis Stanley is a former teacher of English and a graduate student in education. Presently she is the Admissions' Advisory Counselor for the Faculty of Education at Brock University, St. Catharines, Ontario.

David Strahan is Associate Professor of Education at the University of North Carolina at Greensboro. His areas of specialization include adolescent development, curriculum and instruction, and teacher education. He has written over 40 professional articles, co-authored two major middle-school monographs, and is past-editor of *Middle School Research: Selected Studies.*

John Van Hoose is a Professor of Education at the University of North Carolina at Greensboro. His areas of specialization include adolescent development, supervision, and teacher education. He has written numerous nationally refereed publications and presented at over 45 national educational conferences.